JOB HUNTING
FOR PILOTS

JOB HUNTING FOR PILOTS

Networking
your way to a flying job

Greg Brown

Second Edition

Aviation Supplies & Academics, Inc.
Newcastle, Washington 98059

Gregory N. Brown's love for flying is obvious to anyone who knows his column, "Flying Carpet," in AOPA's *Flight Training* magazine or has read his other books, *The Savvy Flight Instructor* and *The Turbine Pilot's Flight Manual.* Mr. Brown has flown professionally in both scheduled and corporate aviation, holds an ATP pilot certificate with Boeing 737 type rating, and a flight instructor certificate with all fixed-wing ratings. He was 2000 Industry/FAA Flight Instructor of the Year, winner of the 1999 NATA Excellence in Pilot Training Award, and the first Master CFI designated by NAFI. In addition to writing extensively on pilot careers, Mr. Brown has lectured on job search techniques to graduating students at Embry-Riddle and Purdue universities and has taught numerous seminars on networking for pilots.

Job Hunting for Pilots: Networking your way to a flying job
by Gregory N. Brown

First Edition 1995. Second Edition 2001. Third Printing (of Second Edition) 2006 by Aviation Supplies & Academics, Inc.

© 2006, 2001, 1995 Gregory N. Brown.

Aviation Supplies & Academics, Inc.
7005 132nd Place SE • Newcastle, WA 98059
Email: asa@asa2fly.com • Website: www.asa2fly.com

Printed in the United States of America

2010   2009   2008   2007   2006   9 7 8 6 5 4 3

ASA-JOB-HUNT
ISBN: 1-56027-624-X , 978-1-56027-624-1

Library of Congress Cataloging-in-Publication Data:
Brown, Gregory N.
   Job hunting for pilots / Gregory N. Brown. — 2nd ed.
      p.   cm.
   1. Air pilots. 2. Aeronautics—Vocational guidance. 3. Social networks I. Title.
TL561.B76 2001
629.132'52'023—dc21   2001002395

To all those pilots who sit around the crew room with high hopes, . . . *until realizing that the people who get the jobs always know somebody.*

Contents

Final Approach: The Interview, 131

Rotate! Getting off the Ground, 153

Happy Landings!, 189

Preface

Sitting Around with Friends, Discussing the Job Hunt . . .

We've all been there—sitting around with friends, discussing the job hunt. Usually talk begins when someone has reached a milestone: a rating or some number of hours that may lead to a job. Then discussion turns to what it *really* takes to get a good flying position. Next, everyone tells the hows and whys of friends who have actually gotten hired.

Sooner or later the same thing always happens . . . somebody tells a story about a pilot who "knew somebody," who got a great job with even fewer hours than the rest of us. As everyone listens in horror, story upon story follows, each about someone who got a job through a contact rather than by merit. Eventually everyone gets upset and leaves.

Why are these "lucky break" stories so disturbing? Because it seems logical that employers would appreciate all the money, time, and energy we've invested in our careers? One would hope that all hiring occurs strictly on merit. It just doesn't seem right that some folks get hired strictly because they know someone.

Maybe it's also disturbing because the path to a professional career seems so straightforward at the outset: earn your ratings; build some flight experience; send out a few resumes; and get hired. But then, as you wrap up your credentials, you find that life isn't quite so simple. Job hunting turns out to be a drag for all but the most fortunate of us. Often it seems that only the "lucky ones" can achieve really good flying jobs anytime soon. Worst of all, those same lucky ones often seem to be less qualified than we are.

What do the rest of us do? The tendency is to buckle down and work harder on building hours . . . and send out more and more resumes. It's easy to see why most of us become drudges where the job search is concerned, and focus exclusively on building credentials.

The fact remains, however, that as long as minimum qualifications are met, the people doing the hiring would rather employ acquaintances than someone unknown. Even with better qualified people out there (like you or me), it's easiest and quickest to hire the known quantity. Even "friends of friends" are pre-screened to a degree. And let's face it, you can't blame your friends for finding jobs through personal connections. If you were the one getting the break, would you turn it down and defer to someone more qualified?

The moral of this story is simple. Along with building professional credentials, you need to make contacts who can help you advance your career. The trick is to be a top-notch professional in your field—and be out there networking at the same time!

The good news is that it's easier (and lots more fun) getting out there and meeting people, than spending your life mailing out resumes with no response. You'll need to develop your skills for meeting people and presenting yourself. There are simple ways to strike up a conversation, to make a good impression, and to stay in touch without offending anybody. There are great places for meeting professionals in your field, and simple methods for enhancing your resume while you're doing it. It takes a little time, and you'll need a system, but the process is fun and rewarding.

The purpose of this book is to share some of these networking skills, thereby allowing you to take control of your career once and for all, and increase your rate of climb. New in this edition is the extension of your networking techniques to include tools of the information age.

The goal is to make you the *subject* of the next job-hunting gripe session—rather than one of the participants!

Acknowledgments

I am grateful to many people for their help and inspiration during the development of both editions of this book. Mark Holt, Jean Brown, Chris Sis, Jeff Helms, and Mark Jagow were kind enough to review drafts and provide suggestions for enhancements.

I appreciate the advice, stories, and anecdotes shared with me over the years that have directly or indirectly inspired me in writing this book. Thanks specifically to Bruce Papier, Tom Payne, Dean Whittaker, O.J. Alexander, Uwe Goehl, Kevin Brazeal, Jim Hackman, Bill Cheek, Gwen Ledbetter, and Kerry Vesper, along with many others not mentioned here. Thanks especially to Jim Thal for conclusively proving that nice guys do make it.

Thanks to Alan Strachn of *Trade-A-Plane* and to "Phil," wherever he is, for use of the marvelous ad shown in Figure 1.1. I am also grateful to Tim Moran for modified use of his letter as an example, to Jim Crail for modified use of his resume, and to Steve Lofgren for his unceasing support in promoting the value of this book for career advancement.

Finally, I'd like to thank Dr. Charles Ahlstrand, Director of the Career Center at Embry-Riddle Aeronautical University–Prescott, for inspiring me through his leadership in developing broad-based job-hunting methods for his students.

JOB HUNTING FOR PILOTS

1

Preflight:
The Groundwork

The Best-Qualified Pilot Always
Gets the Job . . . Right?

From our earliest days as pilots, each of us has learned to revere flight hours. Somewhere back in ground school was buried the subliminal message, "The pilot with the most hours is the best . . . the pilot with the most hours is the best." Strictly from the standpoint of experience, perhaps there's some truth to this. But the question we're considering here is a little different: "Does the pilot with the most hours always get the job?"

Probably everyone reading this book wishes for some additional shoo-in credential for the next job up the career ladder. Single-engine pilots crave multiengine time. Multi pilots want turbine hours. Turboprop pilots want jet time. New flight instructors wish they had their IIs (instrument instructor ratings). Copilots yearn for PIC (pilot-in-command) time. Let's face it, few pilots ever feel that

1.1. Sometimes it seems like pilots can never have perfect credentials for the job. (Ad courtesy of *Trade-A-Plane*).

they've got ideal credentials. Yet people do get jobs, and not always with the best qualifications. Why?

Let's consider the credentials of the two pilots shown in Figure 1.2. One has recently completed all of the basic ratings; the other is quite a bit more experienced. For purposes of job hunting, which of these two individuals would you rather be?

I suspect that if we took a tally of everyone reading this, 99 percent would rather be Pilot B. (The remaining 1 percent would choose Pilot A because they think this is a trick question.) Pilot B is certainly more experienced and of course it's always desirable to have the best experience and

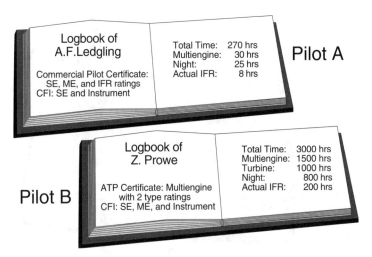

1.2. Pilot qualification comparison.

qualifications possible. Besides, there are a number of flying positions that only Pilot B could hold, due to federal aviation regulations and insurance requirements.

Unfortunately, there aren't many secrets to transforming someone from Pilot A into Pilot B. It's time consuming, difficult, expensive, and often traumatic to pick up those extra few thousand hours, and it takes years.

So is Pilot A's situation hopeless? Maybe not. Let's take another look at Pilots A and B, but with one new distinction added (see Fig. 1.3). Now, who would you rather be? I've talked with plenty of pilots, and almost everyone agrees that Pilot A is often in the better spot.

Surely you've seen those "Position Wanted" ads, where a senior pilot with six jet type-ratings and 10,000 hours is begging for somebody (anybody!) to recognize all that experience and offer him or her a job. Pilot B could be in that position.

At the same time, each of us knows someone like Pilot A who cinched a Learjet position, or was hired by a

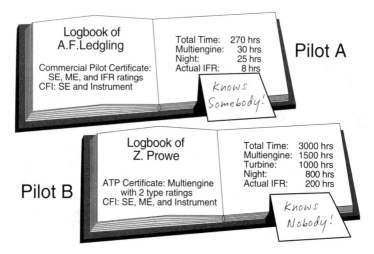

1.3.   Pilot qualification comparison II.

regional airline on a "wet" commercial ticket, or who made it into the "majors" with relatively limited qualifications.

The difference is simply that one pilot "knew somebody," and the other did not. One can either despise the person who got the break, or work hard to be next in line.

Most pilots are goal-oriented. They work hard to build flight time and credentials, and they believe that these added qualifications will make them more attractive as professionals and employees. The fact is, given the number of motivated and experienced pilots, it's almost impossible to become so well qualified that, by virtue of experience alone, you're assured of getting the specific job you want.

That's why you must work just as hard to make good contacts as to earn your ratings. *It's much easier to get to know somebody than it is to collect several thousand additional hours of flight time!* Of course, the best situation is to be well-qualified as a pilot, *and* have contacts who can help you meet your career objectives.

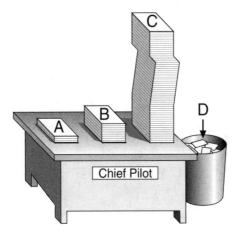

1.4. The chief pilot's desk.

THE CHIEF PILOT'S DESK

Not convinced that connections are important? Perhaps you feel that you already have the qualifications to get hired. Let's check out the chief pilot's desk at Av Ventures, the company where you'd really like to work (Fig. 1.4).

Assume that Av Ventures is interested in hiring a class of pilots. The chief pilot has started by asking a few respected friends and associates for recommendations. Those resumes are in pile A. How many would you assume are in that stack? Five? Twenty?

Pile B holds resumes submitted by current pilots of the company. The chief pilot has put out the word that some hiring will take place and that current employees may submit candidates. (You may be interested to learn that at many companies pilots are limited to two or three hiring recommendations per year.)

Pile C is composed of all those resumes mailed in "cold" by aspiring pilots meeting the minimum qualifications. How do you feel about your odds when in that pile?

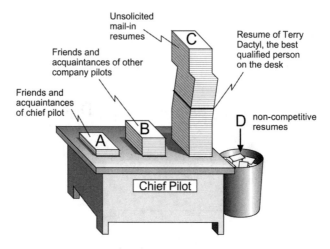

**1.5. Best resume on the chief pilot's desk.
Will this pilot get hired?**

There also is, or I should say was, another stack of resumes. Pile D was composed of all those pilots who did not quite meet some minimum qualification. Even if only a few flight hours short, those resumes ended up in the trash.

Now let's talk about the best-qualified pilot candidate on the desk, Terry Dactyl. Terry has all the right hours and ratings, great references, and a flawless background. This pilot perfectly fits the company's personality profile, is a fine person, and outqualifies most other applicants on the desk. Terry's resume arrived unsolicited by mail, and is highlighted where it landed in pile C (see Fig. 1.5). Is Terry likely to be hired? How about get an interview?

It's pretty obvious in what order the stacks will be processed. Applicants who know the chief pilot or are referred by close friends will certainly get an interview. Friends of the company's line pilots have a fighting chance.

But without such contacts (especially in a noncomputerized system), the odds start looking pretty bleak for those in pile C, including our friend Terry.

One other observation is in order here: there may be a resume or two on the desk for pilots who do not exactly meet stated hiring minimums. If so, those resumes will be found only in piles A or B. The poor souls courting pile C had nobody to lobby for them.

Now please repeat after me, "The pilot with the most hours is not necessarily the one who gets hired . . . the pilot with the most hours is not necessarily the one who gets hired . . ."

Understanding the Odds

Let's look at the job search in another way. When you set out in search of a position, you're a salesperson. If you meet up with a company that's hiring, and if you can sell yourself adequately, that company will "buy" your services in the form of employment.

Every experienced salesperson knows that selling is a numbers game. There may be many prospects out there for a sale, but only so many will have the desire, the need, and the money to buy at any given time. This is actually a fairly predictable situation given any particular product at any particular time. Let's look at some typical figures from the experts—salespeople.

Figure 1.6 reflects some typical sales ratios for fairly major purchases. Please note once again that a flying job requires a purchase (by an employer) just like any other sale.

It Takes →	Cold Calls	(or)	Qualified Prospects	(or)	Referrals →	to make One Sale
	Number of "cold calls" required to make one sale		Number of "qualified prospects" required to make one sale		Number of "referrals" required to make one sale	Number of sales
Cameras	20		4		2	1
Cars	30		5		2	1
Real estate	20		5		3	1
Encyclopedias	30		7		1	1
Cellular phones	12		3		1	1
Flying jobs	?		?		?	1

Cold Calls: Contacting anyone who could possibly be interested;
for a flying job, going to every aircraft operator and knocking on doors.
Qualified Prospects: Those with the need, the money, and the desire to buy;
for a flying job, approaching only companies who need a pilot, can afford to hire one, and want to.
Referrals: People recommended by friends or business contacts;
for a flying job, being referred for a pilot opening by someone the company respects.

1.6.   Average number of prospects required to make one sale.

Let's say that you're a go-getter and decide to pound the pavement in search of a job. You pick up a listing of aircraft operators and then begin knocking on doors, making phone calls, and mailing resumes. How will you fare? Obviously, with this method odds are that you'll have to contact numerous companies in order to find one that'll offer you a job.

COLD CALLS

These types of random contacts are known as *cold calls,* meaning that they have not been screened in more than a rudimentary way, relative to a sale. Figure 1.6 shows the average number of cold calls required of various salespeople to close one sale. Statistically, the auto sales pro from Figure 1.6 needs to speak with an average of thirty random showroom visitors to make one car sale. If you just start knocking on doors and making telephone calls, how many cold calls do you figure it'll take to get one flying job?

QUALIFIED PROSPECTS

The next column lists *qualified prospects,* or those buyers having what it takes to make a purchase—desire, need, and money. Note that, statistically, while thirty random or cold showroom visitors were required to make one car sale, an average of only five qualified prospects are required to make the same sale.

In other words, the salesperson needs to pitch only five qualified prospects to sell a car, but the same person working randomly must approach thirty cold contacts to sell that same car.

For our purposes in looking for a job, qualified prospects are companies who not only have aircraft, but need a pilot(s), have the money to hire, and are actually looking.

Another aspect of qualifying your prospects is finding out how they do their hiring. For example, some companies consider only candidates who have completed an in-house job application. You can send in all the resumes you want, but they'll never look at you. Other companies accept resumes or applications only during defined "hiring windows," specific date ranges often corresponding to their new-hire training classes. If you didn't know about this, odds are your resume is going to arrive on the wrong day and end up in the trash.

Clearly, *you improve your odds tremendously by doing a little homework to qualify prospects before contacting them.* Invest the time to investigate thoroughly who is (or might be) hiring; then concentrate on those leads. Although you'll still need to work as many job opportunities as possible, it should take a heck of a lot fewer disappointments before one works out.

Most importantly, you should qualify the companies you pursue, in order to make sure they measure up to *your* standards. That's right. For some reason pilots often feel they'll be fortunate to get any job involving flying. But getting hired into a crummy company, or the wrong kind of flying—that's no victory, especially in a seniority-based industry where it's not always easy to get out.

Consider the sorts of outfits you want to fly for before putting your name on the chief pilot's desk: the lifestyle; the equipment they fly; and the compensation. Only when they look to you like great opportunities, are they worth pursuing.

REFERRALS

The last column in our table is *referrals*. Let's say I'm looking for a camera, I have the money, and I'm getting ready to take a vacation. I ask my buddy, the photography expert, where to buy one and he recommends a particular camera store. The odds are one in two that I'll buy a camera there—pretty darn good from the standpoint of the camera salesman.

Now back to aviation jobs. Let's say that you've determined that a particular company is a qualified prospect; it needs pilots, can afford to hire some, and is looking. If you're "referred" in, the odds of getting hired are pretty darn good.

We'll come back to this point later, but note that the higher the level at which you're referred into a company, the better your odds are of getting hired. If you're referred by a line pilot, you've got a shot at a job; by the chief pilot, you've got a heck of a good shot; and by the president, you're in unless you blow it!

QUALIFY YOUR LEADS AND SEEK REFERRALS

What does all of this sales stuff mean to you? To put it in perspective, let's look again at the chief pilot's desk in Figure 1.5.

"Cold call" resumes that arrived in the mail were screened by the staff when they arrived; those found "qualified" for an opening have been put into that huge pile C. If the company has no hiring plans, most resumes went into the trash can.

Those applicants who qualified the company before sending in their resumes know the company is hiring, and that they meet the minimum hiring qualifications. They're still in pile C, but at least they're in the resume pile of a company that's hiring.

But to make it into the short-list, piles A or B, the ones who we all know will get hired first, you have to have been referred in. Again, look what that referral is worth to you!

WORK THE NUMBERS!

The other lesson to be learned from sales professionals is that, the more job prospects you work at a time, the more likely the one you really want will pan out. That's why you must always be working two, or five, or ten prospects at a time. During bad times, it may take many more than that to get a job at all. And during good times, working lots of prospects improves your selection when offers start rolling in. But no matter how good any single opportunity looks, don't coast along waiting for that one alone to work out.

Conversely, you must resist the urge to give up after one, two, five, or even ten disappointments. Most of us don't deal well with rejection. Obviously, if it's going to take ten or twenty employer contacts to get a job, you can't go home depressed after each let-down and wait two months before trying again.

Since job hunting is so stressful for most of us, you'll also have to be very careful in your analysis of why you didn't get any one particular job. On one hand, it's always important to debrief after a let-down (perhaps with some objective friends), trying to determine why a particular job didn't pan out. That way you can do better next time.

At the same time, many of us are inclined to shoulder too much of the blame for failure. "Perhaps I said the wrong thing," or "I'll bet if I'd had another 50 hours they'd have hired me." The fact is that unless the employer had an opening, had money to pay you, was in a hiring mode, found you qualified, and had nobody else waiting in the wings, you didn't have a chance. That's why job hunters have to keep on batting and not look too deeply into the interviews that don't work out.

DIRECT MAIL

Where does mass mailing of resumes fit in? Well with all this talk about cold calling versus qualifying leads, it's time to face the cold hard facts about mass mailings.

Let's say you buy a list of all the corporate and commercial aircraft operators in your part of the country. You labor for weeks to put together a terrific resume and cover letter. You and your "significant other" stuff envelopes, lick stamps, and mail away five hundred packets for your first mailing. How will you fare?

"Nothing in today's mail either, dear."

"But. . . we sent out nearly seventy resumes last month!"

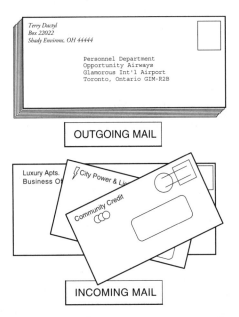

1.7.   Not many replies to your mass resume mailings? Among marketing professionals, a normal response rate to direct mailings is generally considered to be around 1 percent.

To sales and marketing types, this sort of mass mailing is known as *direct mail*. A normal response rate to direct mailings is generally considered to be around one percent. So more than five or six replies, from your five-hundred-piece mailing, is actually an above-average response! What's more, that figure includes the rejections.

Mass resume mailings do sometimes serve to qualify a few prospects. Some companies may send applications or write back with suggestions on when and how to apply. The odds also improve a bit if you do your qualification homework and mail only to those who are definitely hiring.

So, is mass mailing of resumes worthless? If you talk to your friends who've tried it, you probably won't hear many encouraging stories. Certainly if used at all, mass mailings should be part of a much broader job-hunting strategy. Resumes are important; it's just that mass mailings are rarely the best way to use them. (We'll talk more about effective use of resumes in Chapter 5.)

Planning Your Pilot Career

Now let's take a look at your flying career. Have you done any serious planning of the steps necessary to reach your ultimate job? It's important to establish some long-term objectives for yourself, and then follow the "critical path," or shortest, most direct route to your career goal.

WHAT DO YOU WANT TO BE?

Aviation is a wonderfully broad and diverse industry. For that reason piloting offers a wide variety of challenging careers to suit almost any personality. So why is it that one hears only two responses to the question, "What do you want to be?"

The most common answer is, "I want to be an airline pilot," For years, the only civilian flying career recognized by anyone was "airline pilot." And even airline pilots weren't considered at the top of their profession unless commanding a 747 for one of a few specific major airlines.

There were good reasons for this perception in times past. For years airline pilots were the only ones paid a decent wage. They were the only civilians flying relatively safe, all-weather equipment. And, due to stringent hiring requirements at the time (including military training, perfect uncorrected vision, and exceptional physical condition), there was exclusivity in being an airline pilot.

Airline pilot still tops the list as the most popular dream aviator job, partly because of inertia due to the reasons listed above, and partly because airline pilots are among the few aviators regularly in public view. Surveys show that airline pilots are well-recognized as the professionals they are by society. Airline flying is an exciting, well-respected career, often with excellent compensation and benefits. And there are more airline pilot positions than any other kind. No wonder it's the top choice for so many people. Just make sure that if your answer was "airline pilot," you chose it because you've done your homework, and determined that it's the right job for you.

That brings us to the other common answer, "I want to be a pilot, any kind of pilot." This answer implies either lack of industry knowledge, or poor self-confidence that one can qualify based upon anything except luck. "I'll take anything" is one way to interpret that answer.

Well, for any good pilot taking off on a flight, there must be a destination; successfully pursuing a career requires similar planning. I raise these issues because in today's aviation environment, there are so many exciting careers and companies to choose from, each offering its own challenges and rewards. To fully reap the benefits you must take time to learn about different pilot careers and go after the one that interests you most.

Gone are the days when airline captain was the only pilot profession. Today there are also exciting opportunities with cargo carriers. Regional airlines increasingly offer good careers, often flying jets as sophisticated as those of the majors. Corporate pilots enjoy the less structured lifestyle of unscheduled flying, often operating state-of-the-art equipment to international destinations.

Fractional ownership and charter operators offer yet another career direction with rapidly growing pilot opportunity. Even flight training, which was for so long viewed as the bottom of the heap, now increasingly offers excellent career opportunities for those who wish to teach and be professional pilots without leaving home.

Bush flying, emergency medical flying, regional freight, sightseeing—each offers its own balance of rewards and challenges.

The bottom line is that pilot opportunities have never been better for people from all walks of life—people of every race, sex, and age, those who wear glasses, those who have or have not served in the armed forces—to seek and attain flying jobs suiting their particular lifestyles and temperaments.

That's why it's so important, in the course of your job hunting, to investigate properly and choose the pilot career most exciting to you personally, and best suited to your desired lifestyle, no matter what tradition may dictate. That's step one in taking command of your career—set your goal and go for it!

SET COURSE FOR YOUR CAREER OBJECTIVE

Having set goals for yourself, it's now time to plan the route for getting there. Consider the "typical" civilian flying career plotted in Figure 1.8. The career goal shown is jet captain for a major airline, corporation, or charter company, but the same principles certainly hold true for any

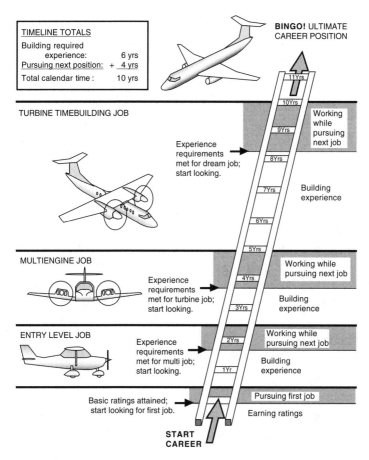

1.8. Typical pilot career ladder. Pilot builds required experience in each job and then starts looking for next career position.

other flying job. Keep in mind that pilot hiring is highly cyclical, so based on the aviation economy at any given moment, and your experience level, your own career sequence and time estimates may vary greatly from the numbers shown in the figure. But the points to be made are the same regardless of when and where you climb the ladder.

When the steps on the figure's hypothetical career ladder are added up, we find that approximately ten years of a pilot's life must be invested to attain that ultimate job. That's a long time. But if you talk with your acquaintances in the business, you'll find that this figure is not uncommon.

Before getting depressed, however, let's make a few observations. Take a good look at the time spent in each job. Note that the typical pilot depicted does not pursue each subsequent job until meeting the minimum qualifications for that next step. You should be asking yourself, "Why doesn't that pilot start looking for each career job a little earlier?"

The problem is that most people tend to get comfortable in their current positions and stay long after they're qualified to move on. Often it takes discouragement or major problems to uproot such pilots and tip them back into the job market. Not until then do they finally dust off the old resume, get back on the phone, and restart the process. This approach is expensive in terms of years spent getting to the top.

Let's see what it's worth to pursue your career a little more aggressively. In Figure 1.9 the pilot still works the same jobs until accumulating adequate experience to move on. But this time he or she has been continually developing contacts along the way, so that the moment each new experience level is reached, the next job is already waiting.

Simply by working in advance to line up each subsequent career job (and without any exceptional luck), note that total time invested to reach the ultimate career has been cut almost by half. This pilot has recouped years of his or her life! Of course the exact time to be saved will vary by individual, but the moral of this story is simple. *Don't wait until you're already qualified to start pursuing your next career job!*

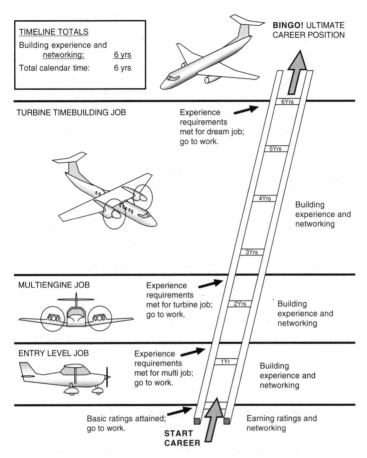

TIMELINE TOTALS
Building experience and
networking: 6 yrs
Total calendar time: 6 yrs

BINGO! ULTIMATE
CAREER POSITION

TURBINE TIMEBUILDING JOB   Experience
requirements
met for dream job;
go to work.

6Yrs

5Yrs

4Yrs   Building
experience and
networking

3Yrs

MULTIENGINE JOB   Experience
requirements
met for turbine job;   2Yrs   Building
go to work.   experience and
networking

ENTRY LEVEL JOB   Experience
requirements
met for multi job;   1Yr   Building
go to work.   experience and
networking

Basic ratings attained;   Earning ratings and
go to work.   networking
**START
CAREER**

**1.9. Pilot career ladder II. Pilot develops contacts
throughout career, progressing to each new job as soon
as qualified.**

THE ROLE OF THE "LUCKY BREAK"

Obviously, no one can promise that your career will
roll along exactly according to either of the time lines we've
just discussed, but the variable is largely in who you know,

and how well you plan. The more good contacts you develop, the better the odds of accelerating your career.

With that in mind, let's consider the jackpot. We all know people who've gotten "lucky breaks." These are the charmed souls who got to skip steps of the typical career ladder because they "knew someone," or stumbled into an unusual opportunity. They're the ones who got hired into turbine jobs with "wet" commercial tickets, the military pilots who went straight to the majors, and those pilots who've made jet captain at a very young age.

Make it a point to talk with some of these people personally (i.e., weed out the ones who exist only in hangar stories). You'll find that in 99 percent of cases, those people somehow actively improved their luck in getting the break.

The contacts you develop to advance your career are the very people who hold the potential for these breaks. In our business, opportunities are always associated with people, and odds require you to meet lots of people to get one break. Think about it. *Lucky breaks are impossible if you don't know anybody!*

SET YOUR SIGHTS ON THE BEST COMPANIES

Any discussion of luck raises one of the big frustrations of pilot job hunting: the sense of lack of control. Those who do nothing but mail out resumes are effectively playing the lottery, hoping that someone—anyone—will respond and hire them. Accordingly, many pilots truly believe that they have no choice of employers; that they'll be hired by whoever will take them. Aside from making people feel out of control of their lives, this attitude has another disadvantage. It removes from each of us the personal mission of working for the best and being the best.

Along with deciding what type of pilot you want to be, a big part of your career planning should be setting sights on companies where you'd truly love to work. Go for reputable, stable flight operations where you'll get good experience, be treated well, and enjoy life as a pilot. Prioritize a list of companies for each career level, with those you'd most like to work for at the top. Do some serious homework on the companies you've chosen, then start planning how you'll go about getting hired there.

You must set the objective of actively enhancing your own "luck," if you want to become the next hangar legend!

2

Best Rate-of-Climb: Techniques for Advancing Your Career

The Importance of "Knowing Somebody"

As you should be gathering by now, this book is about networking. Networking refers to the continuous process of meeting and staying in touch with people who may be helpful and supportive in advancing your career.

How often have you heard the following conversation? A fellow pilot comes rushing out onto the ramp.

"Guess who I just met at the Civic Aviation open house . . . an assistant chief pilot and the training coordinator for Gargantuan Airlines! They were in town for a meeting, and just happened to stop by the open house while I was there."

"That's great. What did they say?"

"Gee, we must have talked for half-an-hour. Gargantuan is gonna be growing like mad over the next eight months. They said to submit a resume and some reference letters right away."

2.1. Internal contacts and references make it easier to get hired.

"Wow, exciting! What were their names?"

"I forgot to ask, but it was a man and a woman, probably both in their forties."

"Do you think they would have personally helped you get on?"

"Maybe. They were encouraging, but it'll be another three months before I've got the hours."

"You'll be qualified in a few months, and you didn't get their names?"

"Well . . . actually I thought about it afterwards. Probably I should have asked for their cards. You don't think I blew a great opportunity, do you?"

THE VALUE OF CONTACTS IN HIRING AT VARIOUS AVIATION JOBS

What should this pilot have done? And where would networking get him or her, anyway? We all know the old cliché, "It's who you know, not what you know." Nowhere is this more true than in aviation. While there are certainly cases where simply mailing in a resume gets someone a job, that's the exception rather than the rule. Where will networking get you? The answer depends, to some degree, on the type of job you're applying for.

Major Airlines. The hiring process for most major airlines is complex and time-consuming. Applicants must submit and regularly update applications, often over a long period of time. Most of the majors use computerized systems to process applications. With these systems, each applicant's resume is quickly screened by a personnel staffer for minimum requirements, then entered into a computer for processing and storage. Applicants are identified for interviews based upon parameters programmed into the computer by the company's employment department.

One might legitimately ask, "What good is networking, when interviewees are selected statistically by computer?" There are several reasons why internal contacts greatly increase a pilot's likelihood of getting hired at a major airline.

First of all, at many airlines it is to your advantage to have a current crewmember carry in your application. Given the crush of applications handled by such outfits, carry-in applications are often processed more promptly than anonymous mail-ins.

Secondly, internal recommendations are important in the hiring process at virtually every carrier. If you are fortunate enough to be accepted for hiring evaluation, recommendations from pilots already employed there are among the criteria that score points. Some airlines virtually require internal references for all applicants.

Finally, even if your inside contact can do nothing else, it's incredibly valuable to have ready access to company information for preparation both of an application and for an interview. A good company contact can access current hiring policies, sensitive topics, and application procedures. He or she deals with many pilots every day and can seek out information from recent hires regarding interviews, sim rides, and the like. In many cases current pilots can also check the status of your application and learn which areas you need to develop in order to get an interview.

Regional or Commuter Airlines.   Hiring procedures at the commuter or regional airlines generally fall into one of three categories. Some use computerized systems similar to those found at the major airlines. A second group hires only through specified training programs, either their own flight training academy, or a specified flight school program. The rest interview based on some combination of internal referrals and evaluation of submitted resumes. The fast-changing regional airline market frequently offers unexpected opportunities to those with "friends" in the business. "We need to find twenty pilots for a class next week," says the chief pilot. "Who knows somebody?"

Corporate Pilot Positions.   Corporate flying opportunities rarely become public knowledge in any formal manner. Corporate flight departments are normally rather close-knit operations. When an opening arises, there is seldom need to advertise. Pilots already in the department have friends and acquaintances who are contacted first. Even if none of these contacts pan out, word of corporate openings spreads through the pilot ranks like wildfire. Rarely will you see an ad for a corporate position. If you do, it's likely for a very experienced and specialized individual. "Wanted, type-rated Captain to fly Citation III. Must have 3000 hours PIC in type and extensive international experience. Preference given to multilingual applicants speaking Swedish and Swahili." Virtually all corporate flying opportunities arise through knowing someone in the department.

An exception to this rule sometimes occurs when a smaller company decides to acquire its first airplane. Purchase of a first aircraft often occurs because a company executive has become personally interested in general aviation, perhaps through taking lessons and getting certified for pleasure flying. Upon realizing the utility and pleasure of personal air travel, the decision is made to start a corporate flight department. In these cases, the executive often begins the pilot search with his or her own flight instructor. If you're a CFI, never turn down a student who is a successful executive or independent professional. Those folks can lead to great opportunities!

Flight Instructors.   There's a good deal of variety in how flight instructors get jobs. Most smaller flight schools, such as FBOs (fixed base operators), tend to run lean operations. They bring in full-time CFIs only when absolutely necessary. Some hire only one or two full-time instructors who are assigned all new students. This approach provides the FBO with the convenience and stability of a professional staff, but creates few opportunities for new hires. Many (perhaps most) small FBOs, however, tend to take the opposite approach. All instructors are part-time or freelance, with each expected to bring in new flight students. This arrangement provides more opportunity to get on with an FBO, providing that the instructor is skilled in attracting new students.

Many flight schools give hiring preference to their own graduates. Given such a policy, outsiders are normally hired only if there is a need for more instructors than there are graduates. The exception, of course, is when an outsider knows the flight school owner or manager.

As you can see, in each of these cases internal contacts and references make it easier to get hired. Many aviation job opportunities are never advertised at all. Pilots must "know somebody" even to learn of the openings. Networking, formally or informally, is how it's done.

Talk with some people who routinely use networking in other professions, such as salespeople and business owners. Service professionals like lawyers and accountants also build business using networking methods. These folks will tell you that the bulk of their opportunities come from networking (or its close relative, word-of-mouth). Flying is no different from other professions in this regard. Knowing someone will help you get hired regardless of your level in the industry.

IS NETWORKING OKAY?

Some people are disturbed by the concept of networking to advance their careers. Perhaps it's because they're afraid of "taking advantage" of people for personal gain. Some feel that they'll disturb people they don't know by approaching them. Others are simply shy or are afraid of making bad impressions upon those they meet. Each of us must work to overcome such feelings because, in most cases, they're simply not correct.

Flying is a business where virtually everyone has received help along the way. Those senior captains at Gargantuan Airlines got breaks years ago that helped put them in pilots' seats. They've had their own mentors through the years, whom they remember fondly. What's more, the sense that "we're all in this together" developed with each bit of assistance that was received. Successful people are generally glad to help others proceeding along the same path.

Helping others makes people feel good about themselves and their own accomplishments. Put yourself in those shoes for a moment. Suppose that you're scheduled for a checkride in the next few days, and have several evenings of studying ahead of you. Just as you settle down to work the phone rings.

"Hi!" says the friendly young voice on the line, "I go to school with your nephew. He told me that you're a pilot, and that you might be willing to speak with me for a few minutes about becoming a pilot myself. Can you help me out?" Would you spend the time to answer those questions? Of course! Who wouldn't? A good deal of pleasure comes from advising someone behind you on the ladder and seeing that person succeed. Other pilots, no matter how impressive their titles, will gladly do the same for you. (Incidentally, don't rule out breaks from people like this whom *you* have helped out; it happens all the time!)

What's more, many flight departments encourage their employees to take an active part in recruiting. Pilots for those outfits are asked to be on the lookout for good, qualified candidates for flight positions. Bringing a sharp new employee on board makes current employees look good, and adds a layer of filtering to the hiring process. For you, meeting such folks could mean a big break. They just need to know that you're out there and looking.

Finally, there's a bit of nostalgia in helping others. As much as any of us may have disliked former jobs, fond memories always seem to prevail later. The people and the adventures of one's early flying days are never forgotten. Even suffering develops some character, once you've moved on to something better! Your mentors are glad to be where they are today, but they'll enjoy reliving their own pasts as they help you up the ladder.

It's important to recognize that over time your better contacts will have invested a fair amount of time and advice in you. If you follow someone's suggestions, a desire develops for that person to see things through, once you meet the qualifications. Think of it as sort of a friendly, implied contract. "I told you to do these things in order to get a job as an airline (or corporate) pilot. You did them faithfully, honorably, and professionally. Now I should help you get hired."

The bottom line is that there's nothing wrong with making friends who will help you along with your career. The important thing is to be discriminating about the people you meet. If they are honorable, ethical people, you can hardly go wrong. Relationships with contacts whom you genuinely like and admire will be comfortable and enjoyable.

You're going to meet valuable contacts and advisors throughout life. Your goals in this regard should be simple. *Meet quality people in your chosen profession whenever you can and then stay in touch!*

Developing Career Contacts

Networking is truly fun when you approach it with the right attitude. The principle is incredibly simple. People always prefer to hire or do business with people they know, or friends of people they know, or friends of friends. Your mission is to tap into this network by meeting people and opening opportunities for them to help you.

As we've discussed, putting forth this effort is just as important as studying for your ratings and building time. Therefore, you'll want to develop your networking skills right along with your flying. I'm now going to ask you to do something that likely will go completely against the grain. *Even if it means missing a few hours of flying, allocate a block of time each week to building career contacts.*

"Allocate" means just that; schedule an uninterrupted period each week in an environment where you can really get something done. It's best to start with a minimum of about four hours per week and go up from there, increasing steadily as you approach each new career qualification. You may well miss a few hours of flying (especially in an un-capped job, like flight instruction), *but it's the only way to move on!*

Let's start with where to meet people who may be able to help you. Then we'll proceed with how to interact with them and how to stay in touch.

BUILD A CAREER CONTACTS LIST

Begin by making a Career Contacts List, a written list of people with whom you'd like to maintain contact. Start with the people you already know, then update regularly with new contacts as you meet them. At least three general types of contacts are found on most people's lists: prospects, advisors, and friends.

Prospects are the folks who, if a job opens up, can actually hire you at a company you'd like to work for. Your Career Contacts List should include outfits where you don't know anyone yet, but would like to; those represent future prospects you'll want to develop.

Advisors or mentors are long-term senior contacts who can help you with advice, and with whom you'll want to

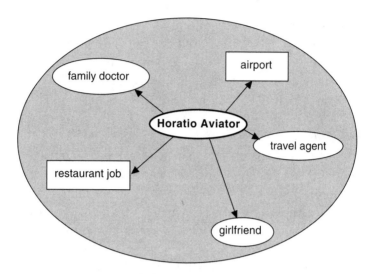

2.2. Many people feel that their own circles of friends and acquaintances are too small to be useful in career advancement.

keep in touch for the future (when you meet the qualifications for jobs at their levels).

For our purposes, friends are people you care for and respect, even if their ability to impact your career is unclear. Friends do sometimes get forgotten. By staying in touch, you sustain the opportunity for one of you to help out the other.

Most people are surprised at the number of contacts they can list at first sitting. If starting a Career Contacts List proves difficult, you may wish to begin by brainstorming with family or friends. It's very important to keep your list up to date as your career progresses. Otherwise, you'll rapidly forget who some of your contacts are and lose touch with them.

Your Career Contacts List will grow rapidly with a little effort. The first step is to call upon relatives and ac-

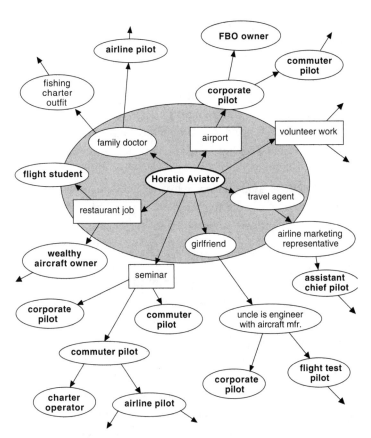

2.3. The principle of networking is to expand your world of contacts through people you already know, along with those you meet.

quaintances to see if they can help, or if they have friends you can contact. Secondly, you'll want to hang around places where chance can work in your favor; where you can meet people and learn of opportunities. Finally, you'll want to develop contacts within specific companies where you'd like to work.

FRIENDS, FAMILY, AND ACQUAINTANCES

Obviously, you'll want to start your Career Contacts List with the people you already know in the aviation business. Next, you must start the detective work of networking by looking for indirect linkages or "friends of friends." Talk with your closest associates: friends; relatives; former employers. Almost everyone has at least a few direct or indirect aviation contacts.

Contact acquaintances who are medical professionals and business consultants. Odds are good that they have patients or clients who are pilots or are in an aviation business. Ask them if they know anyone you could contact for advice.

Do you or any of your acquaintances work for a major corporation or for a subsidiary of a company that operates a flight department? If not, does the organization charter aircraft? If any of your relatives are respected employees at such a company, odds are excellent that they or their superiors can arrange for someone in the flight department to speak with you. (We'll cover what to say later.)

People in the hospitality business (hotels, travel, convention planning, etc.) often have airline, charter, and air tour contacts with whom they work. Those contacts are probably not pilots, but once you're talking to someone in an aviation-based company or department, it's a short route to the contacts you need.

How should you approach these connections? One way is by writing. Mail appropriate letters to everyone you know who might have some good contacts. This includes personal and family friends, relatives, former employers, and community professionals, such as your family doctor, dentist, lawyer, accountant, insurance agent, and investment advisor. The broader the spread of these people, professionally and by location, the better.

The type of letter shown in Figure 2.4 serves several purposes. First, it serves notice that you're actively looking for a position. If your contact actually hears of something, he or she can let you know. Secondly, it challenges the recipient to come up with a few names for you to contact. Letters are read more or less at someone's leisure. The recipient

---

Ella V. Pilot
P.O. Box 3127
Eastern Edge, VA 22334

July 4, 2002

Mr. Finn L. Word
Aviation Consultant
Payne International Airport
Philo, IL 66666

Dear Mr. Word,

It's been some time since we've talked.

As you may remember, I have been working as a charter pilot in Little Rock for the past two years. I now meet the qualifications to be employed as a pilot for a corporation, or for a regional airline. My family is flexible, and I am open to any new location for the right job.

I know that in the course of your work you meet many people of all professions. Can you recommend two or three people I might speak with regarding professional pilot opportunities? Any help you could provide would be greatly appreciated.

I'll give you a ring in a week or so to follow up, if I haven't heard from you in the meantime. I look forward to speaking with you again. Thanks, and regards to your family.

Sincerely,

Ella

Ella V. Pilot

PS: *Jan Golden sends her regards!*

2.4. "I'm looking" letter.

can deal with it when time permits and, if necessary, spend a little time remembering who you are. Finally, many people feel the need to respond to letters. Businesspeople, in particular, tend to put letters in their "to-do" files, as items where action is required.

Enclosing a self-addressed, stamped envelope may be appropriate for contacts other than relatives or close friends; along with demonstrating consideration for your contact's time, it shows that you're seriously expecting a reply.

Many of the people to whom you write will likely respond to your letters. Some, however, will not. Either way, you should plan on following up with a phone call within the time frame stated in your letter.

PUTTING CHANCE TO WORK BY MEETING NEW PEOPLE

Along with tapping people you already know, it's important to open yourself to new opportunities. This is best accomplished by putting yourself in situations where you'll meet plenty of "the right" people.

Meet People On-Line. Thanks to the Internet and on-line networks like CompuServe and AOL (America Online), it's now possible to start your networking without even leaving home. These days almost everybody is active in cyberspace, and pilots are no exception. Accordingly, on-line can be a great place to "meet" professional pilots who can help you along in your career.

Numerous aviation-oriented chat rooms and electronic bulletin boards serve pilots around the Internet, but the service perhaps most accessible for meeting people is AOL.

AOL offers an extensive and well-organized area dedicated to pilots (keyword: Aviation). Not only does this make your life easier in targeting pilot areas of greatest interest to you, but it creates a greater sense of community than other sites, with many regulars hanging around you can get to know over time.

Also helpful is that AOL's chat room format is currently most conducive to real-time interaction. Virtually any time of day or night there are folks hanging around those chat rooms for you to meet, and AOL's member directory allows easy access to profiles of the many members who post them.

The best way to make aviation contacts on AOL, the Internet, or other on-line services, is to hang around dedicated aviation chat rooms, especially the organized pilot forums offered regularly on various topics each week. These ongoing, scheduled forums tend to attract regulars you'll get to know. Also, the nature of conversation there helps you separate the pros who can help you, from other attendees who cannot. This is important not only because you're looking for quality contacts, but also because so many people misrepresent themselves in cyberspace. On the Internet, unlike at the airport, you can't see pilots stepping from their planes, so virtually everyone's stated credentials must be held suspect until you've had the chance to check them out.

Whether on AOL or elsewhere, it's of key importance that you pick a screen name and email address that very obviously project your professional interest in aviation—something like "JetPilot," or "ProAviator." That way everyone who sees them knows immediately that you're a current or aspiring pilot.

Although the Internet should be a useful part of your networking program, it cannot replace the benefits of meeting new people live and in person. This can easily be accomplished through meaningful volunteer work, recreational activities, and certain types of jobs.

Fellow Alums.   Graduates of the same school usually have a strong sense of camaraderie, even if they've never met. Also, school pride lasts forever. Identify other graduates of your school who have pursued careers in aviation. Many university placement centers offer lists of graduates who've indicated a willingness to be contacted for career advice. These people have already said they don't mind hearing from you. Take advantage of their generosity! Such lists and services are generally available to all past students, not just the current crop of graduates. Don't hesitate to drop by, even if it's been years since you attended school.

Also, consider performing volunteer work for your alumni association. These organizations routinely put volunteers on the phone to follow up on alumni. Offer to make some of those telephone calls. People you call will be interested in chatting about what's happening with the program as well as learning whether Professor Smith is still there. Part of your assignment will be updating alumni records as to your contact's latest position. You'll meet some interesting people and learn a lot, while helping out your institution.

College fraternity and sorority members offer particular opportunities in this regard. If you were part of the "Greek system," ask the alumni chairperson from your chapter to find out who among the alums works professionally as a pilot. Those folks are always happy to hear from frat buddies or sorority sisters. Be sure to send regular update letters for publication in your fraternity or sorority newsletter. "I'm currently employed as a flight instructor at Scottsdale Airport and would like to get hired into a charter-flying position. Alumni who can help, please call or write . . ."

Military units also keep track of their former members. Get the names of buddies from your outfit who are working in aviation careers. Don't limit yourself to people you know. Everybody wants to hear the latest about their old unit and to play the "What happened to Joe?" game. You automatically have a lot in common with any of these folks. They'll be glad to extend a hand. Here, again, you may want to volunteer with service organizations where your duties will put you in contact with people "out in the world." Unit service organizations can be good for this, or you can do meaningful work for larger groups like the Air Force Association.

Volunteer Work.   Volunteerism in general is a great way to meet people. Pitch in at air museums. You'll find that many of the other volunteers are professional pilots, mechanics, and prominent businesspeople committed to aviation. Work with the EAA (Experimental Aircraft Association), or with aircraft preservation groups such as the Confederate Air Force and Warbirds of America. Others who volunteer there, and those who own the planes, are again enthusiastic aviation supporters.

Less obvious is that your favorite nonaviation charities are also good places to meet influential people who can help you along in your career. This is especially true when you participate in committee work or corporate fund-raising activities. You'll meet corporate executives and professionals, both working with you on the committee and among the committee's contacts. Similar opportunities arise in chamber of commerce volunteer work (especially for larger communities).

Recreation.   Hit the fly-ins (go to Oshkosh!), soaring (glider), and RC (radio-controlled aircraft) meets. Volunteer to help out at air shows. You're simply not going to have any trouble finding people to talk flying in places like these.

Seminars and Meetings. Professional seminars and meetings are great places to make quality connections. Consider that when you attend, say, a reputable weather radar seminar or one on cockpit resource management, the other attendees will likely be senior pilots or flight managers operating sophisticated equipment. One flyer I know recently attended an engine manufacturer's pilot familiarization course. Every one of the seventeen other attendees was a chief pilot or director of operations!

At the beginning of the seminar, odds are that the leader will go around the room and have everyone introduce themselves. (Be sure to write down the names and companies for future reference.) Be honest about your background even if it's humble. "I drive 152s around the patch at Ruralville Airport." You may get a round of laughs, but all will be impressed by your motivation to move up. After all, everyone else has been in those same shoes at one time or another.

Need more reasons to attend? Not only do such seminars allow you to meet potential employers in an informal setting, but you'll learn something professionally and earn a significant new entry for your resume.

Meetings and conventions of aviation professional groups, such as the National Business Aircraft Association (NBAA), are also great places for meeting important industry people. When attending such meetings be sure to stay at the hotel where the meeting is held and to break and eat with the group. This may cost you a few extra bucks, but meals, breaks, and happy hours offer the best opportunities to break in some really great contacts.

The Airport. Don't ignore the airport! It's always best to fly and work at a cosmopolitan airport where you'll meet people you'd like to work with in the future. Employment in a location where the contacts are limited is far less valuable. If you instruct at an FBO with a charter department and a good clientele of wealthy students and corporate traffic, your odds of moving on quickly are far better than teaching, say, at an isolated flight school with primarily local, private pilot pleasure-flying students.

Whenever an interesting aircraft taxis in at your airport, head over to see it. Ask the pilot if he or she has time to show you around. Hang around the gates of your favorite "someday" airline until you meet some pilots with time to show you the cockpit.

When you fly into a new airport, find out from the most executive-oriented FBO what restaurants are recommended to flight crews and which hotels offer crew discounts. That's where you'll want to go too.

Many airport cafeterias cater to pilots, as do nearby hotel and restaurant "happy hours." Don't feel that you have to drink alcohol at these affairs. Carry around a partially consumed glass of ginger ale, and no one will be the wiser.

Interim Jobs. If you can't get employed as a pilot right away, take a job where you'll meet the right people. (Even if you're already flying, don't rule out something like this for the contacts and some extra income.) If you do a great job working the line for an executive FBO, as a "ramper" for an airline, or as a scheduler for the right flight school, you'll be noticed and valued. Ask any professional pilot who the good rampers are at regular destinations and which ones are pilots. He or she will know! Accordingly, as you build your flight time and ratings you'll be remembered by pilots and managers alike.

Find out which hotels get the majority of the flight crew and executive aviation business, and consider applying for a public-contact job there. Customer service representatives for airport rental car agencies meet lots of pilots, as do the hotel staffers who drive courtesy vans for airport pickups. Many flying professionals frequent the same hotels and restaurants over and over. The ride to the airport is usually long enough that occupants get to know the hotel drivers well over a period of time.

Finally, consider working as a bartender or waiter at a fine restaurant. Patrons will often end up chatting with you about your own life and plans, and you'll learn about theirs. Think of the folks who frequent fine restaurants—many will undoubtedly know someone in aviation who can help you out. Anywhere that such people hang out is a good place to work. Country clubs, golf courses, and vacation resorts are other good spots, along with better hotels. You'll be amazed at the contacts to be made at such places if you pay attention. The numbers alone give you great odds. If one in a hundred customers has a connection and takes the time to chat with you, you'll be able to line up a lead or two a week!

A couple of suggestions are in order about making contacts at these types of jobs. First, always do a *great* job at your work. People do notice and appreciate good work, even if they don't show it. If they're impressed, they'll take time to talk with you and perhaps ask about your job and career. A great contact might come of that chat. But no one wants to refer a lousy employee. Besides, good work makes your employer happy, and a good employer reference is always valuable, no matter what the job.

When the opportunity arises to speak with a customer on a casual basis, make the effort to express personal interest in that person. Obviously, you must be tactful and sensitive so as not to come across as nosy, but people are generally complimented when others ask about their careers, hometowns, and interests.

CONTACT SPECIFIC COMPANIES THAT INTEREST YOU

Developing contacts at companies where you want to work serves both short- and long-term purposes. Obviously, if you're looking for a job right now, meeting people who offer job prospects is the best way to do it. On the other hand, if you're still several years away from qualifying for work at a specific company, inside advisors can be of tremendous value between now and the time you're ready to apply. These folks can help by preparing you for the opportunity, and by laying groundwork for your hiring "on the inside."

Meet Some Pilots. Is there a specific company you'd like to work for but you don't know anyone there yet? Head for the airport! Over time, you should make an effort to meet several pilots who work for every company that interests you. Breaking the ice is easy enough.

"Excuse me, ma'am. I'm a pilot for Ruralville Pipeline Company. My lifelong ambition is to work for Ambrosian Airways' charter department. It'll be a while before I'm qualified to apply, but I'd like to learn more about the company. Do you have a moment to speak with me?"

Ask about aircraft the company operates (you'll probably get an offer to tour one), strengths of the company, and the lifestyle of the people working there. Most pilots are also glad to share information about how they got hired, minimum and realistic employment qualifications for their companies, and the normal hiring process.

Once you're onto these topics, there are three specific questions that must be asked: "What is the best way to approach the company?"; "Is there anyone at the company I should be speaking with?"; and, "May I use your name when I call?" A surprising number of pilots you meet on the ramp will ultimately offer to hand-carry your resume to the proper office, if you stay in touch.

Note names and titles of the company's key people and how best to approach them. Pay particular attention to preferred qualifications and contact procedures. You might expect that these would be the same at all companies, but they're not. For example, some chief pilots prefer to hire "walk-in" candidates who make the effort to visit corporate headquarters. Others hate them!

For another example, some outfits prefer to receive resume and application updates only occasionally (such as every six months or once a year). At others it's best that your name cross a certain person's desk at a certain time each month. Then there are places that should be continually flooded with communications.

Investigate these differences, and incorporate what you learn into your job-hunting program.

The Chief Pilot's Assistant.   Another great place to get information, particularly at small to mid-sized companies, is by calling the chief pilot's assistant. Who's that? We're talking here about the administrative assistant or secretary who handles the chief pilot's affairs. These individuals are good contacts for several reasons. For one thing, they generally know about everything going on in the flight department. Secondly, they know company hiring procedures. In fact, in small to mid-sized companies, they often handle the details personally. If you've been unable to get the answers elsewhere, this is the person to ask such questions as, "How do you review resumes?" "How often and in what manner should I update?" and "Are certain times of the month or year best for keeping in touch?" In short, "What is the best way to keep my file active?"

The chief pilot's assistant is usually easy to reach, and can refer you to other key people in the company. (Again, be sure to ask for permission to use his or her name when calling others.) If such individuals are helpful and encouraging, as they often are, write a note of thanks for their time and advice. These people often do the brunt of the work in their departments and receive little recognition. A gracious thank-you may be remembered one day when resumes are being reviewed.

"Hey, what about that Horatio Aviator guy? Shouldn't he be on the interview list?" If particularly helpful, add the assistant to your contact list for occasional follow-up. It's great to have someone on the inside who you can call once in a while with a question.

Walk-Ins. At many small to medium-sized outfits it pays to visit the company in person. This can be a tough call because many companies will tell you that they don't like walk-ins. It's hard to separate those who truly want no visitors from those who simply don't want too many visitors. The best approach, generally, is to meet some company pilots at the airport first, and query them on the subject. Try to get the name of someone who doesn't mind visitors, and then show up as a referral from a pilot.

When you're in the area anyway, it's probably worth chancing a visit. If you're tactful and considerate it's unlikely that anyone would hold an unannounced visit against you, while on the positive side there's the distinct possibility of making some friends. Who knows? You might even hit the jackpot. "You know that guy who no-showed for new-hire ground school this morning?" says the chief pilot to his assistant, "Well, this woman just walked in and she meets all the qualifications . . ."

When you do elect to visit unannounced, be sensitive to the reception. If everyone is decidedly cool, take the hint and depart—without leaving a resume if anyone appears perturbed. Keep in mind, however, that one job of a receptionist is to screen visitors. Ask to see your party in a courteous and friendly way, even if the receptionist is discouraging.

Perhaps most importantly, know who you want to speak with and a little about the company before showing up. It's just plain tacky to walk in and ask for "the chief flight instructor," or "someone from personnel." Know the person's name you want to speak to, and ask for that specific individual. If you are then directed to someone else, that's okay. (The same goes for mailing unsolicited resumes and letters; call the company and get a proper name and title. Envelopes addressed "To Whom It May Concern," or "Employment Department" often go straight to the circular file.)

Again, the best place to get a contact name is through another company employee, such as a pilot you've met at the airport, or the chief pilot's assistant. That way you also get a referral name. "Captain Martin of the Houston station suggested I stop in and see you." A call to the receptionist or company operator from a nearby pay phone will also do the trick. Sometimes you can find names and titles just by keeping your eyes open; look for a corporate directory in the lobby.

The chief flight instructor for a large FBO told me an interesting story about a fellow who spent half a day "hanging around" the flight school lobby. He read all the materials at hand about the FBO, chatted politely with the receptionist, got a taste of how business was conducted, and familiarized himself with the facility.

The next day he reappeared, this time neatly dressed in a business suit. He greeted the FBO's receptionist by name, having chatted with her the day before, and asked if he could speak with Mr. Hackman, whom he knew to be the chief flight instructor. The applicant was ushered in with no questions asked, politely spoke with the chief CFI, and asked about the possibility of a flight instructor position. "Of course," Hackman told me, "from his previous visit he already knew everyone's name and position at the FBO, his face was familiar and friendly, and he was resourceful. If only I'd had an opening at the time . . . I would have hired him on the spot!"

PRIORITIZING YOUR CONTACTS

We've talked a good deal up until now on the topics of how and where to meet people. But who should be contacted first? In fact it's easy to see that your Career Contacts List may rapidly grow so large that it requires trimming. You'll need to continuously prioritize your list over time, based upon each person's importance to your effort, helpfulness, and position. Priorities may also shift based on who's working for companies that are hiring, versus those on the downhill slide.

To illustrate one particularly important priority among your contacts, let's reconsider your own career ladder. You're obviously going to need to develop contacts all along the way. But resist the urge to start with the contacts at the lowest level and work your way up.

Always emphasize the *highest* level contacts you've got. If your goal is to fly for a specific major airline, start with the most senior pilot or administrator you know at that airline. That senior contact has traveled the whole route, knows the pitfalls and shortcuts, and has broad valuable advice.

Also, he or she has met many people during a long career and has numerous contacts that could be of great value to you. Such a person likely knows people at good corporate or commuter flight departments. Many successful airline pilots even own their own flight schools and charter businesses.

Next, remember that *your best references are those passed from the top down.* It's obviously better to be referred to the company president by an old friend who's a senior airline captain, than it is to be referred from the bottom by the company's newest employee.

Finally, if your goal is to work with that senior pilot one day, you'll want to *set your professional objectives right away.* Among the biggest dangers as you proceed down your career path is losing sight of your goals. If that happens, you're in danger of getting stuck in a go-nowhere job because it's easy, or taking unproductive side trips without realizing it. Although it may be years before you meet the hiring qualifications for your dream position, *find out from that senior captain what you'll need to get hired there, write it down, tack it on the wall by your bed, and go for it!*

Those senior advisors are key to your plans. You'll want to keep in touch with them, inform them as you reach each career milestone, depend on them for advice, and have them waiting to sponsor you at each step along the way.

GETTING AND USING ADVICE: WHAT TO SAY TO YOUR CONTACTS

One of the problems with using words like *contact* and *advisor,* is that, in your mind, they may tend to dehumanize the folks you meet. The "contacts" discussed so heavily in this book are just folks like you and me, perhaps a step or two further up the career ladder. If in doubt about how to approach people, just put yourself in their shoes. How would you prefer to be approached by someone you don't know?

Obviously, you can't easily charge up and yell, "Hey, hire me!" You can, however, display your enthusiasm about the aircraft and the company. Most pilots are delighted to show off their aircraft and can talk all day about flying. Such discussions can sometimes lead in only a few moments to surprisingly direct questions. "Boy, I'd love to work for a company like this. How would someone pursue a position here?"

The trick when meeting new people is always the same: ask good questions and listen to the answers. Most people love to talk about topics that interest them, and everyone loves a good listener.

The easiest and least traumatic reason to contact someone is for advice. When asking people for advice, you are recognizing their accomplishments and station in life. Advice is something that may be given freely and under no obligation by people you meet. What's more, as the person doing the asking you're not expected to do much talking, be particularly confident, or to "know it all." In fact, the best manner to use when approaching your contacts for this purpose is courteous, respectful, and with humility. That's great because those characteristics fit the way most of us feel when approaching a successful professional we don't know.

Two questions in particular are at the heart of the entire job-hunting process. You might as well start working them into your psyche right away! They are:

1. If you were in my shoes, what would you do to get to where you are now?
2. Do you know anyone I should be talking to?

What Would You Be Doing Right Now if You Were in My Shoes?

This question is important because it cuts to the heart of advice you need from your contacts. It is incredibly effective in bringing out specific focused feedback on what to do next. The whole message goes something like this. "I plan to hold a job like yours one day. Here's where I am now. If you were me, what would you do to get there?"

Sometimes it helps to rephrase the question in several different ways. "What was your career path?" and "What kind of flight experience do you recommend I pursue to qualify?" Listen carefully to the answers; then follow up with questions on the specifics. Even if you choose not to take the advice, you will be made aware of issues that your advisor finds critically important.

For those contacts working at "ultimate career companies," there's another specific question. "What kinds of pilots does your company hire?" Take careful notes, and then keep in touch until you are one!

Do You Know Anyone I Should Be Talking To?

This is the single most important question of networking. Once you've spoken with someone, gathered opinions, and formulated a plan, it's time to act. If your contact has suggested pursuing a charter job, ask if he or she knows anyone in that business. If not, does he or she have any acquaintances who might be able to help with information or contacts?

Most people will gladly share their contacts with you, as long as you come across as considerate and "for real." The only trick here is to determine when and if the question should be asked. (Anyone who's ever been on a date has faced much more ticklish issues than this one.) The worst answer you'll receive is, "No, I don't know anyone in that business." Even in that case, don't be surprised if you get a call a week or two later with the name of a subsequently-remembered contact.

One particularly good time to pop the "Do you know anybody . . .?" question is when you meet a prospective employer who is helpful and friendly but has no openings. These people will often graciously refer you directly to another operator—if you remember to ask the question! Don't expect people to offer. Amazingly enough, many people never even think of referring you to someone else unless you bring it up.

The objective is to be able to make a phone call. Remember the chief pilot's desk in Figure 1.5? We're shooting for one of those two referral piles! "Mrs. Smith? This is Horatio Aviator. I was referred to Cheery Charter by Captain Apple of Ambrosian Airways. He says that yours is one of the best companies in the business, and that you might be able to share some advice about getting into charter flying."

GETTING THE BALL ROLLING

Now's a good time to put all of this together in the form of a scenario. Let's say a corporate jet taxis in to the FBO where you instruct. How would you get to know the captain?

"Hello, Ma'am (or Sir), your airplane's a beauty! Would you happen to have a few minutes to show it to me?" If she's not too busy, you'll likely get the grand tour. Most pilots are enthusiasts. Ask some good questions about the equipment, the avionics, what it's like flying corporate, and so on.

If the captain has been friendly and is someone you like and respect, briefly explain your status. "I'm a professional pilot, too. I'm instructing now to build experience, and hope ultimately to fly jets like you do." Ask briefly about the career route she took to reach this professional position and what advice she'd recommend for you.

If the advice sounds good and the captain expresses interest in your situation, ask if she'd be willing to spend a few moments reviewing your resume for comments and suggestions. (Asking for a tour of her flight department is another good way to go.) Do not carry resumes with you for this purpose! Rather, request the captain's card so you can mail a copy. That way you'll have her name and address in your possession, along with a reason for future follow-up.

Within a day or so after your meeting, send the captain a thank-you note for the time spent showing you around the airplane, along with your resume for professional advice and comments. Note on your calendar when you mail the materials, and then follow up with a telephone call two or three days after it should have been received.

By the nature of their jobs pilots are gone a lot, so it'll probably take several calls before you actually connect. What's more, they sometimes spend very little time around the office doing paperwork. So be patient if the captain hasn't yet had time to look over your resume when you call. Explain that you know she is busy, and then together arrange "a good time to meet" (or call back) when there will have been time to look it over.

Once your contact has had time to review your resume and you get together to discuss it (personally or on the phone), pay close attention to suggestions and comments. Hopefully, you've been talking to several people at the same time, and can integrate their suggestions in a useful manner. Remember that the resume is ultimately your own. While your intent is to learn from these folks and gather information, how you actually implement their advice is up to you. You'll likely be sur-

3/9

Dear Captain Apple,

Thanks for showing me around your jet's "front office" yesterday.

Ambrosian Airlines is for me the ultimate career job. It was a big thrill learning more about your company and aircraft.

My resume is enclosed, as promised. I look forward to hearing your suggestions next week after your Antarctica trip.

Have a good flight!

Sincerely,

Horatio Aviator

2.5. Thank-you card.

prised at the quality of information you'll pick up through this process, whether it relates directly to your resume or not.

The whole point here is to get a dialogue going that will help you learn more about how best to pursue your career path. "If you were in my shoes, what would you be doing right now?" "What kinds of positions do you suggest I pursue?" "How much flight time will I need in order to qualify for a job like yours?" Of course, you should always ask, "Is there anyone you'd recommend contacting for those types of positions?"

During or after your meeting, you'll want to write down a few things. Along with information about the equipment and the company, note your new friend's background and any special interests that she expressed. (You'll forget this information more quickly than you think, if it's not recorded—and it'll be useful to you later.) Don't hesitate to make notes on the spot; most people are honored when you find their comments worth recording.

Include the career steps your contact describes and the flight experience required to advance at each step. Note particularly the specific qualifications and hours required to work at her company.

After your meeting, it's imperative to send another thank-you note. (Of course this isn't too much! Have you *ever* heard of anyone getting upset about receiving a thank-you note?) A copy of your updated resume should follow when it's complete.

By this point a good deal has been accomplished. In addition to gaining new insights into your chosen career, you've made a new acquaintance who may be able to help you in the future. Furthermore, you have gotten to know each other well enough so that you can, with a little work, sustain and build that relationship over time.

Don't think of this scenario as a script to memorize. Rather, it's a matter of developing the right attitude about meeting people. When thoughts cross your mind, act on them.

"I wonder how that young pilot got to fly a great airplane like that?" Go say hello and find out!

"Gee, I'd love to work for that company. I wonder how to get on." Go ask the pilot!

"I wonder what it's like to fly a rocket like that one?" Go meet the astronaut and find out!

Make the effort to meet people because you're interested and it's fun. When they turn out to be long-term career contacts, all the better.

3

Flight Following: Keeping in Touch

The Right Place at the Right Time

Most of us find it difficult to keep in touch, even with our closest friends. Distances are great, letters take time, and telephoning is expensive. Email has helped, but many people are too overwhelmed to answer it. This communication problem is further complicated by the differing schedules kept by busy people these days.

Despite these challenges, you want your contacts to think of you whenever an interesting opportunity arises. Therefore it's critical that you remain visible enough to be remembered, at least every month or two. Let's consider for a moment why this is so important.

Back in Chapter 1, we casually examined some of the statistical aspects of job hunting. Another such factor to consider is timing. After all, the major part of "luck" in getting a great job is *being in the right place at the right time.*

Every one of your prospects is (or was) hiring at one time or another. If you walk into virtually any company on exactly the right day, you'll get hired. It's that simple! The problem, of course, is that the odds of showing up at precisely the right time are slim. On the day you walk in, the company may have all the pilots it currently needs. Budget problems often beset flight organizations for long periods of time, resulting in limited staffing. The state of the economy has a huge impact upon hiring.

Flight departments often sit on ambitious growth plans for months, or even years. Then one day a staffing crisis occurs, and pilots must be hired overnight. You know who gets the positions: people on the inside track for jobs, plus the few lucky souls who happen to stumble in the door on the right day. We've all had the horrible experience of talking to a prospective employer one week after this great opportunity. "Oh my, if only you had called a week ago. You would have been perfect for our space shuttle captain slot."

How do you set yourself up for these great opportunities of timing? Let's say that you're making cold calls one day and reach a particularly accessible and friendly chief pilot, Mr. Bill Cheery of Cheery Charter. "I'm afraid we're not hiring right now," he says, "but I've got a little time tomorrow afternoon. I'd be glad to show you around if you'd like to stop by."

You take advantage of this offer, and find that the two of you hit it off right away. Mr. Cheery is a good guy— sharp and friendly. The company appears to be an excellent employer; facilities and aircraft are immaculate. The two of you have some interests in common, and it's obvious that you've made a good impression. In short, this is a place where you'd love to work.

After a great afternoon, the chief pilot escorts you to the door. "You're a well-qualified pilot," he says, "and the type of individual we like to hire. Unfortunately, we rarely have openings. No one's left in years. Thanks for coming by, and good luck!"

Consider this. If one of that company's pilots quits tomorrow, will Mr. Cheery give you a call? Odds are pretty good that he will. Will he remember you after one week? Maybe. After a month? Ninety days? Probably not.

The same is true of your other contacts, fellow pilots, and advisors. If a job opportunity comes up, you'll want to be remembered, even though some time has passed since your first contact. That opens the door for calls like this. "Say, Horatio, this is Bill Cheery. Remember our discussion a few months ago about charter flying? Well, I just got a call from an old friend of mine . . ."

As we've discussed, the odds of walking in on a hiring day are slim. But if you can maintain a presence and a positive impression for a month, your odds improve. Is the job something you'd be interested in after six months or a year? If so, you must be remembered.

Keep your name floating around the offices of your best prospects for a good while after the first call. When the next hiring emergency occurs you may just find yourself on the inside track!

Setting Up a System

Keeping your name alive requires a system, built around your up-to-date Career Contacts List.

You'll need to set up a filing system, where you keep track of communications with your contacts, as well as resumes and applications sent out. For many people, the most convenient way to do this is with files in a file drawer, perhaps supplemented by a personal computer database or contact management software. (See Personal Computers and Job Hunting in Chapter 7.)

CONTACT INFORMATION SHEET

Each time you meet someone new, make a few notes about his or her position, company, and any specific interests that person may have. Some people set up card files for this purpose while others do it by computer or keep notes in a binder. In any case, if you're communicating with more than three or four contacts you'll forget a lot about them if you don't keep notes.

If possible, note any hobbies or interests your new contact has, especially any the two of you have in common. Pay particular attention to comments made about family and children. Just about everyone is proud of his or her kids. It's great to be able to ask intelligently about someone's family when you speak in the future (see Fig. 3.1).

CONTACT TRACKING SHEET

Next, make up a contact tracking sheet (see Fig. 3.2). You'll want to list each of your important contacts along with a check-off column for each month. This is again well suited to tracking by computer using contact management, database, or spreadsheet software. You'll need to determine how often to be in contact with each person on your list and check off the tracking sheet with each communication.

Make it your goal to touch base with each of your current contacts about once per month. For casual or long-term contacts, once every two or three months will be enough to keep you remembered if you need to call. How-

Capt. Jill Byrd   Lear Captain
Chief Pilot
Blue Flight Corp.
111 Easy Street
Carmel, CA

Nice person! Showed me her company's Lear 55, and
gave me lots of great advice (see attached notes.)
Couldn't promise anything, but encouraged me to
send a resume to review now and submit one
formally to her when I reach 750 multi. Possible
opening next spring. Also suggested that I contact
her old squadron mate, Capt. Bill Big, now senior
capt. at Gargantuan AirL. OK to use her name. Told
me to "Stay in touch. Come visit any time." *Yes!!*

*Loves old Corvettes, has two, including split-window coupe.
Into gourmet cooking. Has 3 kids in grade school---ski fans.*

10/18	*Met at Lafayette, IN*
10/20	*Sent thank you note and my resume to review*
	(copy in file)
11/2	*Called to follow up. Jill out 'til Tues am. Bill*
	Smithke answered her phone. He knows my old
	friend, G.I. Flywell. Told me G.I. now flies for
	Geargrinder, Inc. "Say 'hi' when you call him."
	(started separate card for Bill)

3.1. Contact information sheet.

ever, those people are a lot less likely to think of you if a surprise opportunity comes up.

TOOLS FOR KEEPING IN TOUCH

We've already discussed how to get an initial dialogue
going. Now our objectives are to stay in touch and to be remembered for that future eventuality.

Contact Tracking Sheet

Contact Dates by Month, 20<u>02</u>

Contact Names	Jan	Feb	Mar	Apr	May	June	July	Aug	Sep
Capt. Apple, Ambrosian Airlines	✓	✓	✓		✓	✓			
Mr. Elwood, Ethereal Airways	✓	✓		✓	✓	✓			
Ms. Jill Byrd, Blue Flight Corp.		✓	✓	Ph.	✓	Ph.			
Mr. Bill Cheery, Cheery Charter	✓		✓		✓				
Ms. J. Golden, Opportunity Arwys.	✓	✓		✓	✓	✓			
Finn L. Word, Aviation Consultant	Ph.	✓	✓	✓	✓				
Fred Light, F. Light Instruction	✓	✓		✓	✓				

3.2. Contact tracking sheet.

Most of us are appropriately sensitive about calling someone important each month and asking, "May I have a job?" There are, however, some effective, low-key ways to keep in touch casually. Most take very little time to execute.

Holiday Cards.   You can't go wrong with holiday cards. Most people are glad to receive such cards and take them only in the spirit of the season. Just be sensitive to avoid any religious connotations unless you really know the person. You might offend someone who is not a Christian by sending a Christmas card, but no one would likely object to "Holiday Greetings," or "Happy New Year." Be sure that cards are tasteful, because not everyone's sense of humor is the same.

Magazine Articles.   Another good vehicle for this purpose is the magazine article. Any time you read something that might interest one or more of your contacts, make some copies. Jot (directly on the article, so your name will be saved with it) a friendly note, like, "Hi Bill, thought you'd find this interesting." Sign it with your full name, attach your business card (if appropriate), mail it away, and check off your tracking sheet for the month.

Articles are great for a number of reasons. If carefully selected, they show that you know a little about your friends' interests, which everyone finds flattering. You're certainly asking for nothing when you send such material. At worst, the recipient will just think "nice thought," note your name, and throw your article away. At best, you'll brighten someone's day with news of real interest.

Subscribe to a variety of interesting publications that might be good sources. Articles on aircraft your contacts fly and on the companies they fly for are obviously good places to start. Technical and business publications often provide relevant articles, especially if you receive some that not everyone gets. Travel articles can be appropriate, if you know your contacts' regular destinations. Certain popular publications are great for offbeat articles. The *Smithsonian* magazine and its associated publication, *Air & Space*, for example, run interesting articles on a wide variety of topics. As you get to know your contacts better, you'll become more aware of their interests and hobbies, offering more topics for pertinent articles.

For particularly helpful friends and advisors, consider sending a magazine gift subscription as a thank-you. Gift subscriptions are greatly appreciated, but at the same time are not overly extravagant. Best of all, your contact will be reminded of you each month when the magazine arrives!

Postcards and Greeting Cards. Postcards and greeting cards are also great ways to keep in casual contact. Neither requires (nor allows) enough writing to take much time. Postcards obviously also save postage. Finally, have you *ever* gotten a postcard you didn't read?

Be on particular lookout for interesting cards relating to aviation, and when you find good ones buy a supply for future use. Postcards depicting exotic airports and interesting aircraft always catch people's eyes, as do cards featuring appropriate humor.

Every few months, or whenever you reach a professional milestone, be sure to include in your communications a few words about your career progress and accomplishments. When possible, tie your progress to suggestions you received from the person you're writing to. "I broke 500 hours today, 10 percent of my way to Gargantuan Airlines!" or "Here I am in Timbuktu! You were right—charter is a lot of fun." People always enjoy learning that you've heard and understood their comments and taken their advice.

Getting Attention with Your Mail. Every one of us looks forward to our daily mail, until we find out that there's nothing personal in it. Try to make your written communications look personal and interesting, even before they're opened. Buy aviation-related stamps when available. When they're not, look for something else bright and colorful. Selection of an interesting stamp is a personal touch not found on most mail. (Avoid using a postage machine under any circumstances!)

Consider having a rubber stamp made of your favorite airplane for use on envelopes. This can be done at many print shops—just bring in a picture or drawing. One fellow I know sends packages to his contacts wrapped in obsolete aeronautical charts. You can bet that his packages get opened promptly!

Email Communications. Email is a double-edged sword for keeping in touch, mainly because sending it requires so little thought. Properly executed, email can serve nicely for some of your monthly communications. But so much of what comes by email is junk, that many readers automatically delete virtually everything that's not clearly from someone they know. There's also the question of whether recipients mentally register and remember email communications as well as they do a thoughtful item arriving by snail mail (postal service).

For these reasons email should be used sparingly except when you have a real conversation going. Any email you send should be as carefully worded and personal as anything you would send in the mail. That means avoiding forwarded humor, chain letters, and the like which at best are ignored and at worst may annoy the recipient.

With these factors in mind, what makes a good email for occasional use in your monthly contacts? Industry information is appropriate, on those occasions when you learn something your contact may not have heard. Emails are ideal for asking opinions and technical questions, since your contact can answer them at his or her leisure without the interruption of a phone call or the need to write a letter.

Finally, emails can be great for sharing interesting flying stories and destinations you've experienced. Carry a digital camera in your flight case, so when you see something interesting you can take a photo for quick attachment to your email communications—sort of a cyber postcard.

The bottom line is that email is best alternated with other forms of communication, especially for contacts you don't know very well. Every email you send as part of your keep-in-touch strategy should have a specific purpose and message. It should be written just as formally as a note you would send through the mail, and of course, spellchecked.

Otherwise you won't look like a pro—something that just won't do when you're job hunting.

Career Progress Updates. As part of your regular contact process, resume updates should be sent periodically with a casual note attached. Without some career-oriented communications each year, one doesn't look professionally motivated. What's more, your contacts will not likely recognize your career progress if you don't keep them informed. They'll just remember your credentials based on the last time they talked with you. Given today's fast-paced climb up the career ladder, a few months can make a world of difference in your employability.

Another reason to provide updated resumes is so your contacts always have a relatively recent copy at hand, which they can pass on to others should the opportunity arise.

Incidentally, a great way to send resumes by email is in the form of PDF (Adobe portable document format) files, which can be read by anybody having the free Adobe Acrobat Reader on their computer. What's special about PDF files for resumes is that they retain all that formatting you worked so hard to achieve, regardless of the kind of computer or software operated by the recipient. The resume can be printed and look as good as something right off your own printer. Also, the PDF resume can easily be forwarded to others who might be interested in your credentials.

Telephone Calls. Phone calls are a little tougher to inject into the keep-in-touch process. It's important to talk with your contacts periodically to keep the human connection alive. On the other hand, your best contacts are usually busy people. You won't want to bother them too often with unnecessary phone calls.

A good balance is to telephone or make an appointment to visit at least once every few months. Have a specific purpose in mind when you phone. More than the occasional "How're you doing?" call makes you a pest. After you've identified yourself, calls should always open with the question, "Is this a good time to call?" If it is not, "What's a good time to call back when you can speak with me for a few minutes?" Note the answer and act accordingly.

Advice is always a great reason to phone. "I've got a choice between a single-engine turbine job and a multi-engine piston job; what do you recommend I do?"

Important industry news or issues relating to your contact's company are also good reasons to call. "I noticed that your company just acquired an expanding commuter operation. What's the story? Is it somewhere I should apply? Who should I contact?"

Regardless of the stated purpose of the call, be sure to ask friendly questions and show an interest in that person's activities and opinions. (Be sensitive to how much time they have available to talk.) It is always best to keep discussion of yourself and your own situation to a minimum, especially if you have little specific news to report. All you may have to say about yourself is, "I've been working hard to build hours, flying C-340s around the Northeast. My goal is to get my ATP in six months or so." That's fine.

Concentrate most of your call on good questions and truly listen to what your friend has to say. You'll be impressed with just how much industry information, technical knowledge, career advice, and interesting philosophy can be gained through these casual calls to your contacts. And in the process you'll be thought of and remembered.

FOLLOW UP ON ADVICE YOU RECEIVE

It's surprisingly important to let people know when you took their suggestions, and what resulted. People are complimented when someone acts on their advice. More often than not, when giving what we feel to be good advice to others, it's ignored. That's why there's so much pleasure in seeing someone take your advice and benefit from it. If nothing special results upon taking their suggestions, your advisors will often try even harder to help out.

Sharing the outcome of advice shows courtesy and gratitude to the person who gave it to you. It says in essence, "I appreciate the time and expertise that you shared with me. I acted on it, and here are the results." Knowing that their time is not wasted, you're a lot more likely to get continuing help from your advisors in the future. Besides, this sort of follow-up note or call serves as another contact in your "stay in touch" program.

REACTIVATE OLD CONTACTS

Right now you may be thinking to yourself, "Gee, now I realize that I should have stayed in touch with that pilot I met a year and a half ago." It's not too late! Just because you haven't been in touch doesn't mean your contact won't want to hear from you. Old acquaintances may be "dusted off" by letter or with a phone call (see Fig. 3.3).

The nice thing about writing a letter is that the recipient has time to recall who you are without being put on the spot. Your contact may remember even the most casual meeting, but if not, don't worry about it. Along with a reminder of how you met, your letter should provide enough information about your objectives so that your contact can help you, even if he or she doesn't remember. (After all, if

---

Horatio Aviator
Professional Pilot
1313 Palm Lane
Albany, AK 99999

May 28, 2004

Mr. S.W. Elwood
Ethereal Airways
Big Airline Airport
Juneau, WI 55555

Dear Sam,

    I'll be pleasantly surprised if you recall who I am.
We spoke almost two years ago while I was working at
Superquiet Corporation. You had called for information
about our noise-canceling aviation headset.
    At the time we conversed about your position with
Ethereal Airways and about my flight training. You advised
me to send my resume to you once I had attained my
Commercial ticket, and kindly offered to carry it into the
office for me.
    Well, I have completed my training, and although my
hours are still pretty "green," I still have my heart set
on a professional pilot's position. I know that a lot of
time has passed, but any advice you might share, or
contacts you would allow me to utilize would be very much
appreciated.
    How is all going with your career? (Hopefully you are
Captain by now!) I appreciate any response you might have.
Thank you.

Sincerely,

Horatio Aviator

Horatio Aviator

PS: I'll give you a call next week to follow up. We'll see
    if you recognize my voice!

3.3. Letter to reestablish communications with an old contact.

the two of you got along well upon first meeting, why
should this time be any different?)

    The same thing can be accomplished by phone. The
trick is to introduce yourself as if you won't be remembered.
Odds are that you *will* be remembered, but the introduction
will allow your friend a graceful way out if you're not.

"Hello, Captain," goes the call, "This is Horatio Aviator. We met about a year ago on the ramp at Lafayette, Indiana. You were kind enough to show me around your Learjet at the time. I wondered if you might have a few minutes to speak with me, either now or later this week. I'd appreciate your opinions about what's going on in the industry right now, and what I should be doing to position myself."

CARRY THE BALL TO STAY IN TOUCH

Sometimes after long periods of networking the question may arise, "Why do I have to do all the work of staying in touch? I've called and written to this person for a year now. She (or he) always seems glad to hear from me and is always helpful, but never writes or calls unless I make the first move."

This situation is normal and even expected. First of all, successful people are busy. If you catch them at the right time, they'll speak with you freely, but often they're tough to reach or have other things on their minds. Another factor is that older people rarely pursue younger ones and successful people don't usually pursue those still climbing the ladder. How often would you expect a senior airline captain to phone a young charter pilot and say, "Hey, let's get together again, buddy!" Not often, I'm sure you'll agree. The onus almost always rests on the more junior person to stay in touch. It's expected and should be no cause for concern.

In fact, "carrying the ball" can only help you. Successful professionals always appreciate motivated go-getters. If you handle communications professionally and considerately, your mentors will almost certainly be impressed. Odds are that you have at least one aviation contact waiting right now, who told you to "stay in touch." He or she is expecting to hear from you. Do it!

A Smooth Ride: "Luck" and Alternate Routes to the Pilot's Seat

Enhance Your Luck

The best way to enhance your luck job hunting and to keep happy and fulfilled in general is to set some personal goals for your day-to-day life. People will bend over backwards to help others who are hard-working, dependable, and honorable—and whose company they enjoy. It is truly important to set high standards for yourself and to live by them in your dealings with others.

BE HONORABLE

Each of us has met people who claim to have gotten to where they are by deception: falsifying logbooks; exaggerating qualifications; etc. Would you hire someone like that?

One has to believe that no quality organization would knowingly hire such a person and that such people will eventually be found out. Be honorable in all of your dealings. It *will* be noticed and it *will* be remembered in the long term.

BE PROUD OF YOUR ACCOMPLISHMENTS

It's easy to look at others higher up the ladder and feel inferior about your own achievements. If you're instructing in a C-150, take pride in your position and in the fine job you do. People will recognize this professionalism in you, and doors will open. I recently heard from a CFI who had taught a private pilot ground school. Among his students were two teenaged girls who had completed his course and then passed their writtens with high scores. My friend received an enthusiastic call afterwards from their father, who turned out to be a senior captain with a major airline. "What can I do to help you out?" he asked. You just never know how and where opportunities will arise.

DO YOUR BEST TO ENJOY LIFE

Each of our lives has enough challenges to keep us perpetually worried if we allow it. Yet no one wants to hang around with complainers. These people are depressing and often come off as losers. Put 100 percent of your focus into positive thinking and making the most of difficult situations. Hang around with upbeat people, and be one of them. Every time you brighten someone's day you've made a new friend. Doors will open.

BE A WORTHWHILE CONTACT YOURSELF

There's a tendency to think of this networking stuff as a one-way street; that's one reason why so many people hesitate to do it. Well, it's not supposed to be that way. Help others out whenever you can. Introduce people who may benefit by and enjoy knowing each other. They'll do the same for you. Many of the favors you do for others will never be returned—but you'll be surprised at some of the good things that happen to you.

LOOK LIKE A PILOT!

Now for one of the best but most under-used tips in this book. Always wear something aviation-related if it can be done in good taste. That way, while you're doing your volunteer work, playing a round of golf, or dining at a restaurant, others will know that you're a pilot. Just wearing something flight-oriented shows that you're proud of your career and are approachable about it. T-shirts, hats, ties, and even tie tacks are noticed by those who care. Wear an aviation watch.

Who does care? Pilots are attracted to one another like magnets. Suppose that you've been dragged to a party by your significant other. There's no one you know at the gathering, but you're wearing your jet jockey T-shirt. Think anyone will notice? You bet! If there are any pilots around you'll be cornered in minutes. Even "friends of pilots" will want to talk with you.

Don't feel that you have to display aircraft you're already qualified to fly. Just wanting to fly one some day qualifies you to show off any aircraft you like. If you attract someone who already flies that model, all the better!

4.1. **Improve your luck by wearing something aviation-related, so others will know you're a pilot.**

Even when working other jobs, it's often possible to show off your profession. As a bartender or golf caddie, you may be able to wear a playful aviation tie or shirt. On uniforms and suits, aviation tie tacks and lapel pins are noticed far more often than you might suspect. One newly rated commercial pilot I know travels wearing a sport jacket with an aircraft lapel pin. Other pilots often approach him on airline flights, assuming that he's a "jumpseater" (airline pilot commuting to work). Of course, he clarifies that he is not, but that doesn't prevent two pilots from finding something to talk about.

TAKE GOOD CARE OF YOURSELF

Dress nicely, keep your weight down and appearance clean, and be health-conscious. Healthy, happy people are perceived as winners, no matter what they do. Winners get opportunities.

CONTINUALLY EDUCATE YOURSELF

The competition for pilot jobs is incredibly tough. To be most competitive, as well as for personal growth, you should always be working to improve your knowledge and qualifications. Read all the key professional publications; study and keep up on the latest in aviation technology and business. *Aviation Week and Space Technology* magazine is widely recognized as the news leader of the industry. (Most libraries carry it.) Especially if airline flying is your destination, this publication is a must-read.

If corporate flying is your objective, *Business & Commercial Aviation* is a particularly valuable publication, as it covers corporate flight operations and aircraft in a highly illuminating manner. Other good professional magazines include *Aviation International News, Professional Pilot,* and *Airline Pilot* (journal of the Airline Pilots Association). Some of these are available free to qualifying pilots.

Flight Training magazine regularly incorporates excellent articles on aviation careers, especially targeting pilots at early stages of their profession, while *AOPA Pilot* and *Flying* magazines increasingly cover turbine aircraft systems and the latest corporate jet and turboprop models.

Attend professional presentations and seminars whenever you can. (As we've discussed, seminars have triple benefits: you learn, meet people, and get resume credentials.)

When you chat with that Learjet captain on the ramp, he or she will know by your questions whether you're the kind of person who keeps up on things. To be a professional you have to know what you're talking about. Those who do get the job first.

A college degree is rapidly becoming indispensable if you want a decent job. Everyone knows how difficult it is to earn a degree while working. It may take years, but note that even the words "pursuing degree" will enhance your resume significantly.

HONE YOUR COMMUNICATION SKILLS

Most people aren't too comfortable when speaking with strangers. Yet that is exactly what's needed to develop career contacts and to succeed in interview situations. Communication skills must be learned and practiced just like any other. If your speaking skills are weak or you lack confidence talking with people you don't know, you should seriously consider taking a speech or debate class. It doesn't have much to do with flying, I know, but those skills can advance your career tremendously.

A less formal way to improve your speaking skills and confidence is to join Toastmasters, International. This terrific organization has chapters in most communities. Participants from all backgrounds meet once or twice a week to develop their speaking skills in front of others. Since everyone is there for the same reason, it's a great place to practice public speaking and get useful critiques from a sympathetic audience. You might even make some professional contacts there, as participants come from every background and industry.

Make the effort to meet new people on a day-to-day basis, even when they don't appear to offer career prospects.

Not only will you enhance your skills, but you'll be surprised at how often such folks unexpectedly turn out to be useful contacts. The ability to clearly, comfortably, and professionally present yourself pays off, both when meeting new people and at interview time.

ALWAYS TRAIN WITH THE MOST HIGHLY RESPECTED INSTRUCTORS AVAILABLE

You'll learn most from the best instructors, and a good performance will reflect well on you. These folks will respect you for good work and have the credibility to back you both within the organization and outside. Certain types of people earn respect, no matter where they go. Learn from those people and work to be one.

WORK FOR GOOD COMPANIES

Research the companies you could work for and set your sights for the best. Your reputation and credentials are tied to those of the outfit you work for. It's almost impossible for you to be a shining star if you work for a shoddy operation. Why jeopardize your violation-free record and your pilot certificate by working for an operator who doesn't play by the rules?

Be aware of your employer's likelihood of business success. Almost all flight operations are seniority-based, so your climb up the career ladder is greatly affected by how well the organization performs. If the company grows, you'll advance quickly, your flight schedule will improve every month, you'll fly the best aircraft, and life will be rosy. On the other hand, it's a total drag to have the company fold after you've worked there for two years—one week before your upgrade to captain.

MAKE A POSITIVE IMPRESSION ON CO-WORKERS

Keep in mind that the pilots you work with in any given job are likely headed down the same career path as you. Some will make the move before you, and others will follow you, not necessarily in any predictable order.

Obviously, when your peers like and respect you, they are far more inclined to extend a helping hand when the next hiring class comes up. The folks you work with are among your very best career contacts; don't alienate them.

Put another way, that CFI or charter pilot who flies the plane after you tomorrow, may get on with the majors in a few weeks. Will he or she call you when their new employer next looks for pilots? The answer is up to you.

GO FOR THE JUMPSEAT—FAST TRACK TO THE AIRLINES

Imagine, being able to ride up front and chat casually with the pilots of your favorite airline! *Jumpseating,* for those who are not familiar with the term, refers to the accepted professional courtesy of pilots allowing other pilots to travel for free on personal business, when empty seats allow. Most commonly the practice is extended by and to pilots flying for scheduled carriers, though others sometimes offer it, too.

If regional or major airline pilot is your next career destination, jumpseating is an unbeatable way to develop contacts with the companies you'd like to fly for. Not only can you travel for free, but jumpseating can't be beat for getting your foot in the door. Jumpseating privileges should accordingly be high on your priority list when evaluating companies to fly for at various stages of your career.

When offered the opportunity, *jumpseaters should always request the cockpit jump seat* rather than riding in the passenger cabin. You never know who might be flying the airplane—it could be an interviewer for the company, or best friends with the chief pilot. At a minimum, odds are good that you'll make new contacts, gain an ally, or learn something valuable there.

GET OUT AND DO THINGS

Can you meet anyone if you stay home? Not unless you don't pay your rent! Keep active and visible in the aviation community. That way you'll be remembered if a pilot job opportunity opens up. Be sure to express your career goals and objectives to friends and acquaintances; they need to know enough about your status to help out, and to pitch you to others.

BE AN OPPORTUNIST

It's easy to get comfortable on one of the lower steps of the career ladder. In fact, it's incredible how many great job opportunities are missed because of the nuisance of breaking a lease, the ease of staying in a current position, or "lack of time" to fill out a lengthy application. When an opportunity arises, act immediately and aggressively even if you're uncertain of the job's merits. You can always turn down a new position after it's offered to you, but at least the choice will be yours. Just keep in mind that for most people opportunity knocks only so often. Ignoring the knock could set your career back years.

ALWAYS APPLY FOR JOBS ONE STEP BEYOND WHAT YOU FEEL QUALIFIED FOR

You may not get hired as a Learjet captain if you don't have the type-rating. On the other hand, you'll never skip any rungs on the career ladder if you don't reach high enough. You might be able to get the Lear co-pilot position, even though you only feel qualified for a piston job. Go for it!

TAKE A GENUINE INTEREST IN PEOPLE

If you make an effort to get to know the people you meet, they will generally like you and try to help you. This applies to your co-workers as well as strangers. Next time you're sitting in an airline seat, attending a concert, or out playing golf, make the effort to say "Hi" to your neighbors and take an interest in them if they're receptive. You'll get pleasure out of most of these contacts, improve your communication skills, and occasionally open doors.

BE YOUR OWN PERSON

Up to this point we've talked a lot about soliciting opinions regarding your career path. You'll find that for every good suggestion you receive, there will be ten bad points brought against it by others. Don't let the crowd drag you down. Get everyone's relevant opinion, think it over, and then *do what you think is best*. As long as you remain ethical, there are few irreversible decisions. New opportunities will arise, no matter what road you take. Perhaps most importantly, people will respect you for making a decision, whatever the outcome.

Don't Shoot Yourself Down!

Perhaps these suggestions could just as well have fit under the last section, "Enhancing Your Luck." They're here because, in many ways, the things you do wrong may affect your career even more than those you do right. Aside from actions that put a legal blot on your background, there are also personal mistakes that can hurt. Many flight departments, for example, have unwritten "blackball" policies. If any one pilot dislikes an applicant, the candidate is rejected. (The poor applicant will likely never know why.)

DON'T MAKE ENEMIES

It's incredible what a small world this really is, especially within any particular profession or career. No matter what your personal feelings might be about any one individual, try to keep them to yourself. Always be courteous to and respectful of others. A minor argument left unresolved today could keep you out of your dream job one day in the future.

Occasionally there are serious safety, legal, ethical, or moral reasons to differ with others. Try to handle those cases in ways that won't embarrass anyone publicly. A big blow-out argument never benefits anyone. We all make mistakes occasionally. Other people will appreciate your discreet handling of their errors. Besides, you could be the one who's wrong!

DON'T BAD-MOUTH OTHERS . . . EVEN IF YOU'RE RIGHT

Complaining about others makes *you* look like a loser. And when those "others" find out, someday they may impact your career. The most difficult people to get along with are often the most aggressive ones professionally.

You'll likely run into them again somewhere else. Those few moments of enjoyable gossip about your co-workers just aren't worth it.

DON'T DRINK AND DRIVE OR DO DRUGS

DUI (Driving Under the Influence) or drug convictions will delay or prevent you from getting the flight positions you want. Regardless of whether you're at the application stage, on your job's probationary period, or fully hired, your career could easily be terminated.

The decision goes beyond whether it's worth it to drink and drive or whether to do drugs. Think also about your association with others while these things are going on. If your friends get busted for drugs and you're there—even if you're not participating— you've likely got a problem.

A great deal of time and money goes into a pilot's career, not to mention the emotional investment. The rewards are many. Why risk it all for drugs or alcohol?

DON'T BEND THE RULES IN AIRPLANES

Taking chances or breaking regulations in airplanes is risky to your health, the lives of your passengers, your certificate, and your career. Besides, sooner or later people invariably find out. Word gets around our relatively small aviation community amazingly quickly, which leads to the next suggestion.

DON'T TALK TOO MUCH

Don't discuss mistakes or problems in your background with others unless you legally, morally, or ethically have to. Just about everyone has a background problem or two they're concerned about, be it health, employment history, flying skills, or other issues. Sometimes the problems are real and other times they are imagined. People tend to get together with friends and commiserate about their career concerns. "I'm afraid I won't get on at the airlines because . . . "

Don't fall into that trap! Why publicize a problem that could damage your career? You may need to reveal such problems at interviews or on applications if asked, but you may not get asked. Besides, *an employer may be willing to hire you knowing you have a problem, but not if everyone else knows about it, too.*

Alternate Routes to the Pilot's Seat

There's an old saying that luck just means recognizing opportunity when it knocks. With this in mind, it's always valuable to learn how other people got their breaks. In Chapter 1, we considered the typical civilian pilot "career ladder." While most pilots may follow roughly similar paths, not everyone does.

In fact, one of the best ways to accelerate a flying career is to use your contacts to explore alternate routes up the career ladder. Good alternate career paths are rare and hard to identify (otherwise everyone would take them). About all you can do is keep your eyes open, and then act immediately and creatively when opportunities arise. Following are a few examples of alternate routes (some might call them "end runs") around the traditional pilot career ladder.

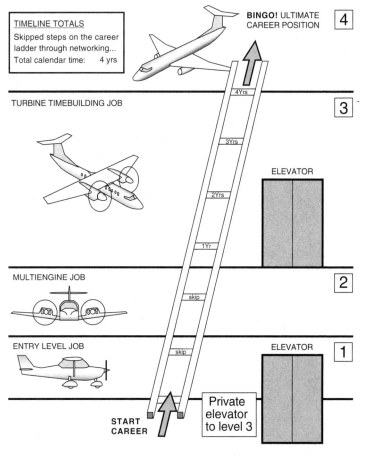

4.2. The "lucky break." Sometimes it's possible to skip steps on the career ladder through one of your contacts or by taking an alternate route.

TRANSFERS FROM WITHIN A COMPANY

Check into transfer and hiring-from-within policies at companies that interest you. Some outfits greatly prefer hiring from the ranks of current employees. One fellow I know was working as an auto claims adjuster for an insurance company when he decided to take flying lessons. The day after he earned his commercial, he walked into the personnel department and applied for a transfer to the flight department. He got it! A month or so later he was flying right seat on a King Air and a Learjet (all this on his temporary commercial pilot certificate).

The same can happen at some large carriers. Not long ago I met an airline pilot who had recently moved into the cockpit after several years working as a flight attendant for the same company. He explained to me that his company prefers to hire from within. Current employees are allowed to interview once per year for flight positions—repeated indefinitely if they so desire—and the hiring minimums are lower for current employees than for outsiders. At least one large freight carrier virtually requires prior experience elsewhere in the company of its new pilot hires.

Do your homework, however, before signing on for seven years as a cabin cleaner in hopes of graduating to a pilot seat. Some companies view internal applicants differently, and have policies discriminating against pilot applicants from other departments in the company. It takes careful research on every individual company to identify opportunities for taking a shortcut.

TRAINING DEPARTMENT POSITIONS

The training department is another avenue into some flight operations. With many air carriers, for example, it's possible to get employed as a ground or simulator instructor with a two- or three-year track into a pilot line. For these positions, companies often hire people with good teaching credentials and communication skills, who appear likely to stay with the training department for some period of time. In many cases, ground instructors may have little or no experience in the aircraft to be taught. The company trains the instructors to teach ground school, usually awarding simulator training positions over time. Many instructors are ultimately type-rated by their employers in the aircraft they teach.

Again, it's important to research the company's policies before signing on the bottom line, as many outfits have no formal transition route from the training department to line pilot, and a few actually require applicants to quit the training department job before applying for a regular pilot seat. In those cases joining the training department could actually set back your objectives of being a line pilot, since ground school or sim instructors rarely get the opportunity to build flight experience in such positions.

SPECIAL SKILLS AND HYBRID JOBS

Most pilots tend to view their employability strictly in terms of flight qualifications. Not all employers see it this way, however. Sometimes a different professional skill or qualification will allow you to override more-experienced pilots for a particular job.

Foreign Language Fluency. For example, the ability to speak multiple languages is of growing value in today's global economy. If you can converse with charter passengers, tourists, or flight students in their native languages, it could help you get a pilot job for which you might not otherwise qualify. The trick is to think creatively as you pursue jobs. "Which of these operators would likely benefit by having a pilot fluent in Japanese and Swedish?" Be sure that such skills are prominently featured on your resume, no matter where you apply.

Pilot/Mechanic.   Many flight departments like to hire experienced AMTs (aircraft maintenance technicians, or aircraft mechanics) for flight positions. These jobs are often advertised as copilot/mechanic positions and allow companies to save money by getting dual duties out of one employee. They are relatively popular with small, corporate flight departments and also with operators who routinely fly to outlocations where little maintenance is available. At least one large jet charter operator requires an A&P (Airframe and Powerplant) certificate of all new-hire pilots.

Pilot/Professional.   Many pilots got their starts in other careers before turning to flying. Professional experience in another field can be a great way to get a job that includes flying duties, but some creativity may be required to make it happen. Attorneys, accountants, engineers, repair technicians, salespeople, and medical professionals frequently hold jobs where travel is desirable or required. As a result, in some cases you may find yourself more employable as some other professional who flies than simply as a pilot.

Positions well-suited to technology-oriented professionals who fly are sales engineers and on-site repair technicians. Medical, dental, and mental health professionals should consider applying to practices that service outlying rural locations on a regular weekly basis. Emergency medical flight operations may be appropriate for those with trauma experience as nurses or EMTs (emergency medical technicians).

Among law enforcement agencies, enforcement experience usually takes precedence over pilot background. Therefore, seasoned officers and appropriately trained military veterans might want to investigate enforcement flying positions.

Traveling sales positions for large-ticket items may also justify use of an airplane. Examples include sales of heavy equipment, scientific instrumentation, and industrial equipment and materials.

Many professional consulting services are also well adapted to use aircraft. Among the more common ones are engineering, architecture, computers and software, contracting, accounting, and management consulting. Clients may be spread over a large geographic area, with the need to fly in several consultants at a time for projects.

In each of these cases, many companies will be delighted to hire someone with professional experience in the field who can also fly airplanes. Keep in mind that with such jobs you may fly fewer hours than you'd like, and perhaps operate something less than your dream aircraft. You'll also likely have to do some work in your "old" professional field. The good news, however, is that you'll probably get treated with respect, make lots of contacts that'll help you down the line, and get paid an honest-to-goodness living wage while you're building flight experience. That's not such a bad deal, is it? Besides, in many companies once the principals get used to the benefits of flying, there is soon interest in flying more hours and moving up to larger aircraft.

To find these types of hybrid professional positions, subscribe to the relevant professional journals and scan the classifieds for jobs well-suited to flying. List your flying qualifications prominently on your professional resume—as a business skill, not as a hobby!

It also pays to invest in professional journal ads of your own, under "Positions Wanted."

> Experienced bookkeeper and commercial pilot seeks
> position where both of these skills can be utilized.

Remember that, although there aren't a great many of these hybrid jobs around, there are even fewer pilots qualified to fill them. Therefore, if you've got the background it's often worth your effort to pursue them.

SPECIALIZED FLIGHT OPERATIONS

Some specialized flying positions offer experience that can substitute for traditional flight qualifications in the move up to more-sophisticated aircraft. One example is scenic air-tour operations. Tour flying requires intimate knowledge of local geography, excellent interpersonal skills, and sometimes familiarity with special regulations.

In Hawaii, for example, and at the Grand Canyon, numerous operators employ hundreds of tour pilots. Most start by flying single-pilot, single-engine aircraft tours. After a few months of tour flying, pilots develop a good deal of specialized knowledge involving routes, regulations, and customer service. As a result, they are often quickly transitioned into multiengine tour aircraft, even with limited prior twin-engine experience.

At the top of the ladder for many sightseeing operators are scheduled turbine-powered aircraft tours. Although pilots may have to switch companies several times to do it, here's a case where taking the right single-engine job can move you through several levels of an aviation career, often very rapidly.

Similar opportunities sometimes present themselves to freight pilots. Many freight carriers operate a variety of aircraft. Piston and turbine singles are used for small package contracts, transport of canceled checks, and the like. Twins and twin turboprops carry heavy, hazardous, or emergency freight loads. Freight jobs often have long hours and difficult schedules, but the flying experience can be terrific, along with the opportunity to move up to larger aircraft within the same company.

Consider charter operators for the same reason. Most offer a variety of aircraft to their customers for different types of missions. It's not at all uncommon for the same operator to operate singles, piston twins, turboprops, and jets. The charter business is often particularly difficult to get into, unless you "know someone." Once you're on the company's "certificate," however, opportunities to move up from entry-level positions into larger aircraft can be very good.

UNCONVENTIONAL METHODS

Occasionally one hears of a pilot who did something clever and unusual to get a job. This is difficult to do well and is often risky business. It's probably safe to say that for every person who's tried something daring and gotten hired as a result of it, many more did something in bad taste and blew it! (Most such stories turn out to be fiction, anyway.)

One unusual tactic that seems to work for some people involves new-hire ground school classes. At smaller companies, pilots sometimes request permission to "sit in" on new-hire pilot ground schools, or in rare cases, even show up uninvited and ask on the spot to attend. This isn't always as crazy as it sounds, because in many cases the situation benefits both pilots and company. The pilot applicant demonstrates eagerness to work for the company, diligence in class performance, and the willingness to invest personal time in attending the ground school. The company gains back-up pilot trainees at no additional cost or obligation.

If any other pilots hired for the class don't show up, or drop out, someone sitting in is already there to take the position. Even if no one drops out, the situation can pay off. If the company suddenly needs more pilots than anticipated (not at all uncommon), those sitting in have already completed ground school. It's a relatively simple matter to complete the paperwork and get on with flight training.

Even if nothing immediate results from sitting in on a ground school class, participants hopefully have learned something and developed good contacts within the company. While drop-in opportunities at major airlines are virtually unheard of, the practice is not uncommon at air taxi outfits and smaller regional airlines.

5

Required Paperwork

Your Resume

Hopefully by now you're convinced that unsolicited mass mailings of resumes is rarely the best way to go. Resumes are most effectively used in a few specific situations. A truly effective job hunter may hand out only a few resumes over an entire career!

The best use of resumes is providing them to contacts and job prospects who've asked you for one. These people already know who you are and have expressed a willingness to help you. They can get your resumes into the all-important referral stacks at your target employers.

Sending resumes to companies with computerized hiring systems is okay—as long as you meet their minimum requirements. Your information is entered into their computers; if all the numbers add up, you may someday get a call.

Responding to ads obviously makes sense, as does mailing to companies that you know are hiring. However, you'll do a lot better in these situations by getting to know someone there first. Then you're back to communicating at a personal level with an inside contact.

THE MISSION OF A RESUME

There are countless differing opinions as to the right and wrong ways to prepare a resume. People argue for hours over whether a resume should have a picture on it or not, over how the "Career Objective" should be worded, and whether or not to use colored paper. The fact is that there's no magic in preparation of a good resume, just lots of work.

The function of your resume is to present your experience and qualifications in the most favorable manner possible. If you follow my advice up to now, you'll rarely be sending a resume to anyone with whom you haven't already spoken.

When a contact receives your resume, the reaction should be, "This individual seemed sharp when we talked. Now I see that her (or his) credentials back up my impression." This perception is very important, because your contacts will be putting their own reputations on the line by referring you for an interview. If your resume doesn't make you look sharp, it won't be forwarded to the right people.

The single mission of your resume is to present your credentials in a manner that will get you an interview. (Note that I did not say "get you a job." You'll have to sell yourself for the job at your interview.) Any resume that gets you an interview for a job you want is a good one!

GENERAL RULES FOR RESUMES

First, a few words about the general information that should go on a resume. Some people get the impression that a resume must be a detailed and complete life history. Wrong! "Resume" means summary, and it need summarize only that information relevant to the desired position.

While a job application may require your complete work history, a resume does not.

In fact, one mistake people make on resumes is putting in too much information. Again, the only information that should be presented is that which will help you get an interview. A perfect resume has all the information that could possibly help you get an interview, but not one bit more! This should become clearer as we proceed.

Almost everyone agrees that basic resumes should be only *one page long*. (Exceptions to this rule are resumes for academic and upper management positions. Even then, one-page resumes are often used for first-time employer contact.)

The general rules of resume organization are simple.

1. *Most important categories go first.* The most important categories on any given resume vary by individual. "Most important" may perhaps be thought of as "most impressive." If your strong suit is Professional Experience, it should be the first category on your resume. Lots of flight hours? List Flight Experience first. New graduates of recognized flight programs, especially those with low time, may want to list Education first. Continue on down the resume from most important (for you personally) to least important.

2. *Within any one category, list most recent entries first.* This is one of the few hard-and-fast rules of resume writing. Under each resume category, entries should be listed in reverse chronological order. Under the category of "Professional Experience," for example, list your current or most recent position first; then work backwards with each job entry to the oldest, which should appear last.

MAJOR RESUME SECTIONS

The information categories of pilot resumes are fairly standardized. After all, everybody needs to present similar basic information in order to demonstrate minimum hiring qualifications (certificates, work experience, flight time, etc.). This basic information must be presented clearly.

There's more to a good resume, however, than just a list of qualifications. Since so many pilots meet the minimums for most jobs, your resume should be crafted to set you above other similarly qualified applicants. This is easier said than done, and is largely accomplished through the details of resume entries. Anyone can slap the basic information onto a resume. The challenge comes in expressing personal attributes such as responsibility, integrity, teamwork, leadership, and the respect of your peers. Every entry on your resume should present some specific skill or accomplishment that makes you special. The toughest part—all of this must fit on one page!

Name and Address. You'd be amazed at how many people have lost job opportunities because their resume addresses were incorrect or obsolete. What a drag it is to learn that you've missed your dream job because the employer couldn't reach you!

Be sure that a permanent address appears somewhere on your resume. If you expect to be moving around, use the address of a permanently located relative. Another option is to rent an inexpensive P.O. box and keep it active indefinitely. (Get a U.S. Post Office box; the private mailbox places sometimes go out of business.) Be sure to file and update forwarding orders as you move around.

Objective. The one objective that must always appear on your resume is the general type of position you're applying for. Employers need to know whether you're applying for a pilot's position or for a secretarial position.

Too much detail, however, can be a problem. As a recent pilot graduate, you might be tempted to put down, "I am interested in a professional flight instructor position where I can gain hours and experience." This tells the chief pilot that you're not asking to be considered for the Citation co-pilot job that just opened up. Might you have been interested?

In most cases all that's necessary is to list "Pilot Resume" prominently at the top of your resume. It tells what type of professional position you're applying for, while excluding you from nothing. Use a detailed "Objective" statement only if you have a very specific job goal, or are targeting a very clearly defined position. (For targeting specific jobs, see Cover Letters, later in this chapter.)

Professional Experience. This is perhaps the most difficult resume category to construct, especially if your background is varied. First, you'll want to determine what work experience is truly relevant to the position you're applying for. Remember that there may be excellent and desirable experience buried even in your non-flying positions.

The public contact skills that come with sales and customer service positions, for example, are beneficial in almost any job. Technical and mechanical skills obviously offer good background for understanding aircraft systems. People and project management skills are valuable both for commanding large aircraft and for interacting with ground personnel. Instructors and check pilots are always in demand; so demonstrated teaching abilities are a plus.

Part of the difficulty in writing such listings is in objectively evaluating your own past positions. People often tend to discount the value of their own experience, especially outside their current field. To tackle this, gather a group of three or four people in your field whom you respect. (Include some who don't know too much about your background.) Ask them to quiz you about your past positions and to help you identify the most impressive skills and experience from each job.

Then with their help, make sure that each position is named in the most appropriate manner possible, with a brief paragraph highlighting the key background drawn out by your "panel."

It's generally not necessary to go back more than five or so years in describing your work experience, unless you see a benefit to it. For example, if you have ten years of aviation experience, it's probably well worth listing. If, on the other hand, you've changed career paths after years in other fields, it may be best to stick primarily with your more recent experience on the current career track. Many years of entries, especially with lots of job variety, may cause you to appear uncommitted, overexperienced, or too old for the job at hand.

Certificates and Ratings. This category should pretty well speak for itself. Just be sure to list your most important current certificates first, followed by the associated ratings. These days it's probably worth noting somewhere in that section if you have "no incidents, accidents, or violations" on your record.

Horatio Aviator

1313 Palm Lane, Albany, AK 99999, (907) 555-1212
Permanent Address: Heartbreak Aviators Hotel, Upper Volta, IN 44444, (317) 555-1212 (after 5/15/02)

OBJECTIVE
A flight instructor or Part 91 pilot service position with a growing company offering advancement potential into multiengine aircraft and/or charter operations.

CERTIFICATES AND RATINGS
Commercial Pilot: Airplane Single and Multiengine Land
Flight Instructor: Airplane Single Engine *(CFII expected March, 2002)*
FAA Class I Medical Certificate: Excellent health, non-smoker

EDUCATION
AS: Aviation Management *(expected May, 2002)*
Outstanding Instrument Flight Student, *Fall Semester, 2001*
Albany Junior College, Albany, AK

FLIGHT EXPERIENCE

Total Time	315	Combined Instrument.	32
Pilot-in-Command	247	Night	37
Multiengine	15		

RELATED COLLEGE COURSEWORK

Aerodynamics	Aviation Meteorology
Advanced Aircraft Systems	Turbine and Piston Powerplants
Maintenance Fundamentals	Aviation Management

WORK EXPERIENCE
Lineman, Sunnyside Air Service, Albany, AK, *9/01 - present*
Responsible for fueling, servicing, and securing aircraft. Managed line supplies inventory. Assisted manager with account records and assisted mechanics on aircraft maintenance. Occasionally flew company aircraft to Anchorage to pick up parts.

Asst. Manager, Photo Department, A-Mart, Worcester, IN, *summers, 2000-01*
Assisted Dept. Manager in sales, ordering, and customer service in a large discount store. Served as Manager-on-Duty on weekends. Employee-of-the-Month three times.

Groundskeeper, Bath Muni. Golf Course, Bath, ME, *part time & summers, 1998-99*
Responsible for all maintenance and mechanical repairs on golf carts and other vehicles, maintained grounds, and assisted in pro shop during busy periods.

OTHER INTERESTS
Dogsled racing, aircraft mechanics, travel, and basketball.

AVAILABILITY
May 15, 2002

2/02

5.1.   Resume of a less-experienced pilot.

Often pilots start their job searches (as they should) before completing all the ratings required. Don't hesitate to list planned ratings on your resume. Simply note something like, "Certificated Flight Instructor: Airplane SE and ME (CFII expected March 2010)."

Flight Experience. This topic is also pretty much self-explanatory. The key here is to not go into excessive detail. Don't list flight time by aircraft type, for example, unless you know for a fact that your prospective employer operates that type of equipment, or you're pretty certain that the time will "translate." It may be hard to believe, but if you list 50 hours in a C-172, a PA-28 operator may not hire you as a flight instructor! Better to lump it all under "Single Engine." If you list 5,000 hours flying Learjets, a turboprop operator may consider you unqualified! Unless it is specifically a Lear pilot position you're applying for, just list your total turbine time, and let the aircraft type show up under "Ratings" and/or "Work Experience."

Also, avoid listing time that's ridiculously low in any one area. For example, don't list "Actual Instrument" time on your resume, if you have only 1.5 hours in the soup. This sort of listing screams, "I have no experience!" Just lump hood, actual, and simulator times under the single heading of "Instrument." The number will be much more reasonable. Do you have lots of turboprop, but only one hour of jet time? Combine them under "Turbine." Let prospective employers ask about that stuff, if they really want to, once you've got your foot in the door at the interview. (In many cases no one will ask.) Just be sure that what's listed is correct and honest.

Education. "Education" is an increasingly important category. If you don't have a four-year degree already, you should be seriously considering pursuing one for most of the really desirable flying jobs. For example, only exceptionally qualified pilots get hired at the major airlines without college degrees. (It doesn't seem to matter what your degree is in, as long as you have one.)

Along with any degrees already earned, consider listing any important studies in progress. These might appear as "Degree Studies in Progress," "pursuing BS in [subject]," or "associate's degree expected [month and year]."

If you attended college but did not finish, make an entry like "General Studies," or "Studies in [field]," and list the college attended. If you have no college whatsoever, consider leaving the "Education" section out of your resume altogether; let your other qualifications do the talking.

Pilots with relatively little professional experience (such as new college grads) may wish to expand their "Education" sections by including specialized aviation course work completed. For example, if you went through a professional or university flight program, classes in advanced equipment, systems, and meteorology may be worth listing.

OPTIONAL RESUME SECTIONS

Professional Development. Space permitting, you may wish to include a section entitled something like "Professional Development," "Special Training," or "Continuing Education." Include such listings as weather radar seminars, crew resource management (CRM) courses, management workshops, and specialized training classes. While such training won't in itself replace experience, it does show that you're motivated and a learning, growing professional. It also allows less experienced and non-degreed pilots to show motivation and professional development that may separate them from the pack.

PILOT RESUME:

Marissa K. Pilot
SS# 123-456-789

1500 Flying Fish Lane
Aquatic Aerie, FL 33333
(813) 555-1212

CERTIFICATES AND RATINGS:
Airline Transport Pilot: CE-550, Multiengine Land
Commercial Privileges: Airplane Single Engine Land
Flight Instructor: Airplane Single and Multiengine, Instrument Airplane
Ground Instructor: Advanced, Instrument
Flight Engineer: Basic and Turbojet written tests completed
FAA Class I Medical Certificate: Excellent health, non-smoker

FLIGHT EXPERIENCE:

Total Time	6690	Actual Instrument	815
Pilot-in-Command	4905	Night	895
Multiengine	2575	Simulated Instrument	175
Turbine	1740	No accidents, incidents, or violations	

RECENT PROFESSIONAL EXPERIENCE:

9/00 - present **Cargo Pilot** — Extraterrestrial Systems, Inc. East Westerly, IN — Fly Citation all-weather over Eastern U.S. Coordinated aircraft purchase, flight & maintenance analyses, and flight scheduling

6/99 - 8/00 **Chief Flight Instructor** — F. Light Instruction and Charter - East Better Days Field, Ghostown, FL — Taught flight and ground school courses at regional FBO. Responsible for all training standardization, FAA liaison, phase checks

8/95 - 2/99 **Electronics Radar Technician** — Illinois Air National Guard Springfield, IL — Lead Radar Technician on McDonnell Douglas F-4D Phantom. NCO of the Quarter two times during service

EDUCATION:
1995 **B.S. Economics** University of Illinois at Urbana-Champaign
1995 **Radar Technician Certification** Radar and Avionics Systems Technology School, Lowry AFB, Denver, CO

SPECIAL TRAINING:
9/00 CE-550 Type Training, Atta Flight Type School, Tuscaloosa, AL
8/00 Physiological Training, including Altitude Chamber, Randolph AFB, San Antonio, TX
5/99 AOPA CFI Renewal Program, Detroit, MI
4/99 ClearVision Weather Radar Operators Course, San Francisco, CA

OTHER ACTIVITIES:
Volunteer, SC Florida Big Sister Program, County Heart Association
Aerobatic competition flying, travel, cycling, hiking, and other outdoor activities

9/01

5.2. Resume of an experienced pilot.

Special Skills. This is another resume section you may wish to include, depending on your background. Foreign language skills, for example, are in high demand these days for many types of jobs. Among them are flight instructors at contract flight schools, scenic tour operators, and charter or scheduled carriers operating internationally. CPR skills,

EMT or other safety certifications may also be valuable to list, along with management, computer, and in some cases, sales skills.

Personal Data. Many people incorporate "Personal" categories in their resumes. Most of what ends up listed there is material that the employer is not even legally allowed to ask. Your date of birth, age, marital status, number of children, and the like are things which should be considered carefully before listing. Your age may be a plus or a minus—depending on how old you are and what the job is. Some companies value a stable family as a sign of loyalty and maturity in applicants. Others worry that married applicants will be unhappy with travel or relocation that may be required in the position. Listing information regarding religion, political affiliation, race, or sexual orientation is rarely a good idea, no matter how proud you may be of them. Why offer anyone the opportunity to discriminate?

The bottom line is, never put any personal information on your resume without careful consideration. If in doubt, leave it out!

Interests. Some experts feel that "Outside Activities," or "Other Interests" should not be listed on resumes. I disagree, so long as potentially controversial interests, like those described above, are not included. In most flying jobs you'll be spending days on end with your employers and co-workers. Given the choice, most people would rather spend all that time with someone interesting.

Under "Interests," try to list one or two leisure-time aviation activities along with some non-flying ones. Pilot employers like to hire true aviation enthusiasts—people who are involved in aviation even on their days off. General aviation flying, soaring (gliders), kit plane building, radio-controlled aircraft, or even scale model-building would fall under this category.

If it turns out that you have some other common interests with your potential employer, all the better. People love meeting others with similar interests. Veterans from the same unit, graduates of the same college, and players of the same sport as yours will be glad to learn of your interests. I was once offered an interview because I played a particular musical instrument the company recruiter was seeking for his after-hours band.

I experienced a similar case from the other side, while serving on a corporate hiring committee. Having interviewed many applicants for a particular job position, the committee had narrowed the field to five equally qualified candidates for the one position. After a good deal of hand-wringing about which person to select, someone noted that one woman under consideration had listed volleyball under "Activities" on her resume. Further review of her application revealed that she had played championship intramural volleyball at the big ten university where she studied. Our company was active in a corporate sports league, and volleyball season was just beginning. Who do you think got hired?

Whether or not your prospective employers share common interests with you, they'll be glad to know that you get some exercise and have interests in addition to your job. Just don't list anything that looks foolhardy. (Who wants to hand over a two-million dollar airplane to a bungee-jumper?) Don't list so much detail that you give the impression that these other interests are more important to you than the job at hand. And again, stay away from listings with moral, political, or religious implications. Odds are slim that your prospective employer feels the same way about such topics as you do.

Finally, note that the title "Hobbies" was not used for this resume section; that word implies amateurism. You'll want to convey seriousness, even in the pursuit of your outside interests. Just stay light enough so that there are no questions about where your main interest lies. Keep listings in this category to a maximum of four or five. In other words, don't list *all* of your sumo wrestling titles!

WRITING YOUR RESUME

Composing resume entries can be very challenging, particularly for those trying to condense many years of experience onto one page. Almost everyone needs help to do this well, especially in refining "Professional Experience" entries. Plan on five or six drafts before you get it right. Call upon knowledgeable friends and associates, as well as those advisors you've been fostering, to help identify your most impressive credentials and experience for your resume.

It's also worth mentioning that for many people, the writing itself is tough. This isn't school, so it's not cheating to get help making your resume read like that of a pro! If you need assistance, consider hiring a professional writer to help refine your resume. Just remember to keep the ball in your own hands when it comes to content.

FIND AND CORRECT ANY MISTAKES

You mustn't have a sloppy layout or spelling errors on your resume. Everybody already knows this, right? Apparently not, because employers will tell you that a large percentage of resumes they receive have significant errors. Most applicants don't do this on purpose; they make mistakes. That's why you must *have several sharp individuals proofread every written communication you send out.*

Many pilots feel that a spelling error here or there shouldn't reflect badly on them. "This isn't a writing job," they say, "it's a flying job!" The fact is that poor attention to detail on your resume implies the same cursory attitude on the job. Typos, grammatical errors, and messiness often guarantee that you won't get an interview. Since flying is a detail-oriented profession, letting mistakes slip by raises questions. Will this pilot miss something on preflight? Will the paperwork be properly completed? Aviation employers want perfectionists for pilots; don't let your resume disappoint them.

THE ROLE OF INTEGRITY

This section on resumes has focused on the importance of conveying pilot qualifications in the best possible light. In discussing resumes, applications, and interviews, it's equally important to point out the role of honesty and personal integrity. Often there's a fine line between favorably presenting real qualifications, and misrepresentation. Most of us know pilots who have padded their logbooks, or who have used other deceptive methods to get hired. All too often they don't seem to get caught.

Nevertheless, personal integrity is perhaps the single most important factor in earning a great job. Employers in all fields routinely make exceptions to hire someone less qualified who is confirmed as honest and honorable. Accordingly, this is a good place to state the need for absolute honesty, both on the resume and at the interview. The problem arises because, in the absence of other information, recruiters tend to hire the people who look most specifically qualified on paper.

This trade-off between personal integrity and looking good on paper can become a problem for job applicants.

That's why it's so important to be totally honest, but to present yourself in the best possible light.

Testing your resume for honesty and effectiveness is straightforward. Once each entry is honed into final form, ask yourself two questions. "Is this entry as impressive as it can be?" and, "If asked about this listing at the interview, will I be comfortable in answering?" If the answers to both questions are yes, you've done a great job. Otherwise, you need to do a little more work.

RESUME ORGANIZATION AND APPEARANCE

We've seen that a significant aspect of your resume is to convey the facts of your background to potential employers in the most positive manner possible. With that in mind, it's important to consider how resumes are reviewed. For any given flying position, many resumes are usually reviewed in a short time. The actual time spent by potential employers on the first screening of a resume probably amounts only to seconds. During those few seconds you must convey all of your key qualifications and make a favorable impression.

Highlighting Key Qualifications. To accomplish these objectives quickly, your resume graphics must be impeccable. Key qualifications in each resume section should be underlined or in bold typeface and should lead off the entry. For example, under "Experience," the most important element in each entry is probably your title (such as chief pilot).

A second level of detail should reflect the company you worked for and the time spent there. Finally, you'll want to include a concise description of your duties.

To test your resume's efficiency at conveying key information, scan it by reading only the bold or underlined phrases. This is what a reviewer will likely do first, only

---

OSCAR P. "HATCH" BOMBAY
19300 Iron Eggs Avenue, Moore, Oklahoma 73160
Voice and Fax: (405)555-1212
E-mail: o.pen.hatch@bombay.com

Objective	**Career Flight Officer, Ambrosian Airlines**

Flight Time   **Total Flying Hours: 3,200**

Heavy Jet:	2,800	Multiengine:	3,000
Pilot-in-Command:	1,200	Second-in-Command:	1,000
Night:	300	Simulator:	500

Certificates   **ATP with B-707/720 type rating expected Nov, 2002**
                                Private Pilot: ASEL, with Instrument Rating
                                FAA First Class Medical   FCC Restricted Radiotel. Permit

Experience   **Pilot, United States Air Force**

                  E-3 Pilot, Tinker AFB, OK (1999 to Present)
                    - Extensive operational experience in Europe and Southwest Asia.
                    - Over 40 combat sorties in support of operations in Southwest Asia.
                    - Earned safety award for skillfully recovering smoke-filled aircraft.
                    - Over 1,000 hours flight experience in B-707 derivative aircraft.
                    - Project pilot on $1.6 billion engine and avionics upgrade.

                  B-52 Instructor Pilot, K.I. Sawyer AFB, MI (1996 to 1999)
                    - Chief, Tactics & Training, developed training for 40 flight crews.
                    - Led top flight crew on wing Operational Readiness Inspection (ORI).
                    - Instructed combat aircrews in world-wide flight operations.
                    - Better than 800 hours in Boeing turbofan-powered aircraft.

                  B-52 Pilot, Anderson AFB, Guam (1992-1996)
                    - Everyday experience in Pacific and SE Asia flight operations.
                    - Outstanding performance on ORI, earned "Best Bomb" award.
                    - More than 1,000 hours in very heavy 8-engine turbojet aircraft.

Education   **Crew Resource Management Training**, Tinker AFB, OK
                    - Including semi-annual simulator refresher training.
                  Cockpit Resource Management Course, K.I. Sawyer AFB, MI
                    - Including annual simulator refresher training.
                  Combat Flight Instructor Course, Castle AFB, CA
                  Bachelor of Science, Eastern Illinois University

Personal   Excellent Overall Health   Non-Smoker
                  Married   Soc. Security Number: 000-00-0000

Available   **FALL 2003**

5.3.   Resume of a transitioning military pilot.

then looking deeper if the applicant seems potentially qualified or interesting.

"Hmmm," says the reviewer upon first scan of your resume, "this guy Horatio is an ATP with 6700 total time, a B.S. in economics, and has experience as chief flight instructor and cargo pilot . . . looks pretty good at first glance." At this point the reviewer will likely go back for more detail in areas of interest.

"Let's see, where did this guy work in the cargo position, and what did he fly?" If that looks good the reviewer will dig even deeper, with an eye towards filling the specific job he or she has in mind.

"I like what I'm seeing here, so far, wonder if this guy has any management experience that could be useful at our Fresno operation . . . let's see what responsibilities he's had in these positions." Now the reviewer is reading the fine print you labored to write, and it appears that you may get an interview out of the deal.

This scenario illustrates why it's so important to take the time to: 1) identify and include all your best qualifications and attributes on your resume; and 2) organize it in a fashion that prioritizes your qualifications in a clear and logical manner.

Resume Graphics.   Another key aspect of your resume is its graphic appearance. The more organized and polished your qualifications look, the better you'll appear to your prospective employer. Professionalism is a big part of what any employer is looking for. While many pilots like to think that applicants are judged only on "facts," the truth is that a favorable first impression may help you win the job over someone with slightly better numbers.

As noted designer Raymond Loewy[1] once said, "Between two products equal in price, function, and quality, the better looking will outsell the other." Given the resumes of two equally qualified applicants . . . well, you get the pic-

---

1. Loewy, Raymond, *Industrial Design*, 1979. The Overlook Press, Woodstock, NY.

ture. Just as it's necessary to dress presentably for an interview, it pays to tailor your resume's organization and appearance so it's among the sharpest on the employer's desk.

To accomplish this, organize your resume for conciseness and readability, and if you haven't done it already, enter it on your computer. If you don't have one, use a friend's, or rent some computer time at a copy shop or library. (Be sure to keep a backup disk, and if you use someone else's computer include details on the type of computer and software used.) Then make a serious effort to fine-tune the appearance of your resume through careful use of layout and type. (Many word processing programs come with templates for this purpose.) The point is to make your resume project your image as serious, sharp, and professional.

If this sounds difficult to you, or if you don't have the equipment to do the job, speak with a graphic designer about helping you with the appearance of your resume. (You can get a referral from your copy- or printshop; some offer the service themselves.) In any case, it's incredibly important that your resume is designed so it'll look terrific every time it's printed out.

Since you probably plan to update your resume often, you may wonder how you can afford to invest so much energy in it every time. The simple answer is that you won't have to. Updates of a properly designed resume are generally quick and easy. You'll rarely be modifying the basic information on your resume. Rather, what will change are a few details like your flight hours, your ratings, and an occasional job listing. You can quickly update such items on the computer and then print out a current resume. (It's helpful to incorporate the date inconspicuously on each new resume you produce, so you can later determine which versions are held by each prospective employer.)

DUPLICATING YOUR RESUME

There are several different ways to duplicate your resume. Obviously, if you have ready access to a computer and a good-quality laser or inkjet printer, you can simply print out as many copies as you need, directly onto your letterhead. (Letterhead refers to the paper with your address that you use for letters. We'll get back to this shortly.)

If you need more than a few copies, another option is to use your computer to print a best-quality "original" of your resume on white paper. This original can then be taken to a copy shop and duplicated in quantity directly onto your letterhead. If you use good-quality copy machines and make certain that the glass is clean before copying, the duplicated resumes will look virtually as good as printed ones and you can produce as many as you need.

For those who, despite my advice, are taking the mass mailing approach, that same white original may be taken to a print shop for offset printing. This generally makes economic sense for quantities in the hundreds. (Be sure to get references on print shops; their quality and service vary tremendously.) Another reason to go to a print shop would be if you want to use colored ink. In that case it's often most economical to print matching letterhead and envelopes at the same time.

PAPER STOCK

Now, about that paper for your resume. It's simply amazing how much paper quality impacts the professional look and feel of your resume. Go to a good quality print shop, copy shop, or stationery store and pick out some paper you like. Be sure to buy something compatible with laser and inkjet printers, as well as with professional copy machines and offset printing. Avoid unusual colors or overly exotic papers. Innovation is, unfortunately, not an overly desirable quality in our business. If you want to set yourself apart, it should be as a confident individual who's right in the mainstream. That's best accomplished through the clarity of your design, and the quality of the paper on which it's printed.

When you buy your resume paper, get enough matching blank paper and envelopes for use in cover letters and other professional communications with your prospects. You can use this same paper for listing references or other information required by some prospective employers. Some applicants go even further. You may wish to copy all of your certificates, letters of reference, and other paperwork onto this same stationery. It makes the whole resume and application packet match.

Estimate the *maximum* number of letters, resumes, reference sheets, envelopes, and other support materials you expect to send out per week or per month. (Be sure to allow for reprinting of resumes as your qualifications change.) Then buy a year's supply or more. Paper and envelope availability varies tremendously; you may not be able to find the same stock next time you need it. Since blank paper is relatively inexpensive, save yourself trouble in the future by stockpiling a good supply.

If budget permits, and you have a permanent address, you may wish to have some letterhead stationery and envelopes printed with your name and address for an even more professional appearance. This printed stationery can also be run through a computer printer or copier for use in resumes or other reference materials.

Cover Letters

The words *cover letter* are often spoken only in hushed whispers by people cowering in dark alleys. As with resumes, many people think that there's some secret incarnation of this simple document that makes all the difference in "getting the gold." (Otherwise, why would everyone be rushing around, copying cover letters from their friends?)

The purposes of a cover letter are simple: to introduce yourself and to tailor the information on your resume to the specific job you are applying for. Your cover letter should be a concise but convincing presentation of why you're a good candidate for the job.

Cover letters should be cordial, professional, and right to the point. If you were referred to the company to which you are applying, name the person who referred you within the first sentence or two of your letter. That name could make all the difference as to which stack your resume is placed in. You wouldn't want anyone to miss your referrer!

It's perfectly okay to send a one-paragraph letter if you have little to say. Doing so, however, puts all the burden of communicating how closely you fit the job requirements on your resume. Don't expect the reader to draw too many conclusions from your resume, beyond the facts presented.

A cover letter offers the special opportunity to bring in additional details about your background that are relevant to the job opening. Think of it as the place to state the reasons why you should be hired.

Take a look at the cover letter shown in Figure 5.4. Although the writer has just earned her CFI, she has other experience that might make her a better instructor than the average applicant. This information is presented in a concise way in her letter. A cover letter allows you to "put a spin" on your resume information, or to sum up and tailor your qualifications to the job in a conversational manner.

Cover letters also provide the opportunity to connect your resume with other support materials that may be useful in presenting your case. For example, if you have special qualifications relative to the specific job at hand, consider including an additional reference page with your resume. In that case the cover letter might say something like this:

> Although I attained my CFI relatively recently, I do have a good deal of varied experience both as a pilot and as a teacher. I feel that this background greatly enhances my ability to perform well in the position of [flight instructor]. Kindly take a moment to review the Summary of Flight and Teaching Experience that I've enclosed with my resume.

A cover letter is the one place where you can make a personal statement about yourself. Use it to bring all of your experience together and to show off your professionalism and communication skills. Most importantly, cover letters offer the opportunity to present yourself as a uniquely qualified individual, even if your numbers look just like everyone else's.

SAVE YOUR COVER LETTERS AND SUBMITTED RESUMES

Cover letters are among the many communications that should be saved for your records. Put them on file, or save them on computer disk. When interview time comes, it's useful to remember what you wrote to a prospective employer. (The open file will be on the interviewer's desk.)

I. Emma Flyer
14325 N. 264th St.
Big City, WA 89898

May 1, 2002

Mr. Fred Light
F. Light Instruction
Papier Sans Serif Training and Balloon Field
Las Vegas, NM 88888

Dear Mr. Light,

As you remember, I was referred by your friend Captain Apple, of Ambrosian Airways. Thanks for taking time to speak with me the other day regarding your Flight Instructor opening, and for sending materials on your operation. I am very impressed with the scope of your training department. Please consider me for a position when the expansion takes place. Enclosed is my current resume.

While I'm a relatively new CFI, please note that I have over six years of teaching experience, both in my position as a community college mathematics teacher, and as a weapons instructor in the Air Force. I also have over five years of flying experience, including significant IFR and night time.

I believe that my combined flight experience and teaching background will allow me to do an excellent job for your company, if I am selected for the Flight Instructor position. I'll give you a call after you return on Friday to see if we can schedule an interview. Thank you for your consideration!

Sincerely,
Emma Flyer
I. Emma Flyer

5.4. Cover letter.

Perhaps even more importantly, a file of cover letters and submitted resumes can save you lots of work. You may be done writing cover letters today, but three months down the road you may need another one. Why start over from scratch? There's no need to create a brand new letter each time. Most people end up with three or four basic letters that can be modified slightly to send with each resume or application.

Business Cards

Order some business cards to use both in making contacts and with your stationery. Your local print- or copy-shop will have card stock available to match your resume paper. Business cards are valuable for a number of reasons. Properly executed, they present you as a professional, rather than a "wanna-be." When opportunities present themselves, you can provide key contacts all of your information in a concise manner. (Upon meeting people you'll no longer have to write your name and address using lipstick on a napkin.) Business cards can also serve to remind your contact a little about you as a person, long after your meeting.

On your card, you'll need to list a mailing address and phone number where you'll be reachable for the foreseeable future. If a second "permanent" address is necessary, don't hesitate to list it.

Also prominent on your business card should be your email address. If you don't have email, then you'd better get it. These days email is the preferred method of communication for many people you'll meet. Not having it forces them to phone or send a letter, which for some is just one more obstacle to contacting you. Besides, email, unlike postal addresses and telephone numbers, can instantly follow you wherever you move. Even if you don't have your own computer you can establish an email address on that of a friend or relative. But having such an address is imperative. While we're on the topic, make sure that your on-line service offers full Internet access, and allows your email address to accept attachments. Increasingly, email attachments and websites are the preferred methods of sharing employment information. If you have set up a relevant Website, you should list it on your card as well.

Titles and ratings? Many pilots like to show off all of their flight certifications on their business cards: "Horatio Aviator, Commercial Pilot, Certified Flight Instructor-Single Engine." But be careful, if you choose to do that. You don't want anything on your business card that might "pigeon-hole" you.

Horatio is telling everyone with that card that he doesn't yet have a multiengine rating; that he's not an instrument instructor, and that he fancies himself as a long-term professional at the CFI level. There's absolutely nothing wrong with that, as long as Horatio doesn't secretly yearn for other opportunities. It's just that by listing what credentials he already has, Horatio is also broadcasting what he *doesn't* have. He could earn his multiengine rating or a CFII in a matter of days, if the right opportunity came along. Might he consider a charter twin position? How about right seat in a turboprop? Depending upon his career status, you bet he might be interested! Put only as much information on your card as you can without ruling anything out. Do you have a B-737 type-rating? Don't put it on your business card if you fancy a corporate pilot position.

There's an old saying among advertising types that the number of words on a business card is inversely proportional to the importance of its bearer. In other words, the more words used to describe a person's position, the less important they are likely to be. Conversely, the President of the United States needs only two words on his business card; a first name and a last name. Keep the information on your card to a minimum.

When it comes to job hunting, many pilots do best by simply listing their name and address on a business card, along with the words "Professional Pilot." That tells the story with no extra connotations, whether you're a Cherokee pilot aspiring to the airlines, a commuter pilot bound for corporate flying, or a military jet jockey seeking a civilian job. When the card is handed to someone, it'll stimulate the question, "Oh yeah? Who do you fly for?" Now, you can tailor your answer to the situation, including laying out your future plans along with your current position.

One other thing to incorporate on your card is a personal photo. Remember that jet captain you met at the airport? He or she may not remember your name, but if you talked in the way we discussed, there's a good chance of recalling your face. If you hand that captain your card with a photo on it (make sure you collect his or hers as well), then, when your face shows up in the mail accompanying thank-you notes, resumes, and follow-up communications, you'll most certainly be remembered.

A business card is one of the few stationery items you can have a bit of fun with. (Don't dare use anything but the strictest formality on a resume or letterhead.) For example, while you could dress up in a flight shirt and tie for your business card photo, you might also consider a photo in casual dress next to a hobby aircraft like a glider, warbird, or antique. An alternative would be a logo, slogan, or appropriate humor if you so desire.

This is okay because you'll be handing your card out in person and attaching it to your keep-in-touch communications. In these cases people will enjoy the informality, plus the personal touch helps them remember you.

Personal Website

Increasingly, these days, people are developing personal Internet Websites to showcase their interests, families, and professions. At this point there's no need to create one exclusively for the process of job-hunting, but if you're doing a Website anyway (or already have one), there are distinct opportunities to use it as one of your job-hunting tools.

Think of it this way. A Website offers the opportunity to concisely express who you are and where you're headed professionally, without boring the people you meet with long stories or endless photo albums.

Obviously you should dedicate at least a portion of your site to aviation interests, since that's what you'll have in common with your professional contacts. It's okay to present other interests there, too, but if the site is extensive you may want to create a special entry page just for aviation visitors. Otherwise, some pilots entering at your "needle-point" screen may never make it to your "flying accomplishments" screen.

A Website is great for showcasing your aviation interests through the use of photos, text, and links; it also allows you the opportunity to post relevant credentials, such as your current flight time and ratings. If you like, you can even post your resume or incorporate a link for downloading it. The trick with Websites, however, is to balance your aviation professionalism with a touch of the real you. If you're into soaring or ballooning or antique aircraft, here's the place to show off those interests, and to share a bit of fun with your visitors in the process. Even esoteric interests can be included—your favorite flying poem might not work on a resume, but it's perfectly appropriate on a personal Website.

Of course, linking a stranger to your Website is in a sense like giving them a key to your home—make sure that the dirty laundry is picked up, risqué photos are put away, and the kitchen is clean! Offer links to your Website only if you can keep it looking nice and working as it should. Properly executed, a Website is great for showcasing your professionalism and attention to detail, but done poorly it could blow your image completely. So build a good one, or don't bother at all.

How will people learn of your Website? Rarely will anyone ask specifically for your web address (URL), but email links and a listing on your business card subtly invite people to drop by at their convenience and see who you are. A surprising number will take you up on the invitation.

Also, opportunities will arise to refer people to your site when you share common interests. For example, glider pilots you meet can be referred to your Website to check out the experimental sailplane you're building. This may not happen often, but when the other glider pilot turns out to be a senior captain at United, the Website will have been proven well worth your effort.

References

Good personal and professional references are perhaps the most meaningful but under-utilized components of the job application process. They are often critically important at the resume screening, interview, and hiring committee stages of the process. Yet few people put much effort into collecting and assembling references. As a result, using them properly can give you a big boost over the competition.

DEVELOPING REFERENCE CONTACTS

Job applicants often think of employment references simply as a list of names filling a slot on a resume, but there's much more to it than that. Pilot resumes often appear very similar, especially in terms of flight qualifications. Once the minimum hiring requirements are met, 500 hours difference between resumes is not of great significance. So among your challenges when applying for a pilot position is to appear more-qualified or better-suited than the next applicant.

Proper use of references is one way to do this. Two factors are important when selecting references for your list: how important your references appear on paper; and what they'll have to say about you.

It's always desirable to list some references having impressive management titles. People in leadership positions such as chief pilot, commanding officer, and company president will be considered well-qualified to judge your performance. Such titles on your list suggest that you can muster some heavy support for your professionalism.

The next issue is what your references have to say about you. At the resume review level, references may be noted, but are rarely called. Checking references is more common at later stages of the hiring process. Obviously, you should select only people whom you know are impressed by your performance.

In my own experience as an employer, I've always been amazed at how many references really don't have much to say about the applicants who listed them. In these cases it is usually clear that the applicant never really talked with them ahead of time.

When considering a person for use as a reference, make an appointment to discuss it. "I'm preparing materials to apply for a pilot position with a regional airline. Do you have any advice for me on the topic? May I list you as a reference?" Listen carefully to what they say, and then come right out with it. "If you got a call from one of those companies, what would you say about me?"

After a joke or two to keep from overly boosting your ego, your reference will generally share his or her comments in an honest manner. You should be sensitive to whether the person really wants to be your reference, and whether his or her comments are, in your opinion, supportive of your position. Don't worry about your references saying something different to an employer than they said to you. If you've picked the proper people, this rarely happens.

LETTERS OF REFERENCE

Reference letters are only sometimes required with applications and interviews and rarely with resumes. However, they're virtually always accepted, and in fact are among your most powerful secret weapons in the job hunt. When you submit letters of reference with your applications, they are almost always read. References provide a powerful opportunity to strengthen your position against the competition.

Good reference letters are not easy to come by. First, you need people who have something good to say about you. Secondly, they must be eloquent and literate enough to say it well in writing. Finally, they must be willing to invest the time to write the letter.

Because of these challenges, collecting reference letters needs to become part of your regular routine, long before any application is actually due. The best time to ask for a reference letter is when you've done something well and made someone happy.

Just aced a checkride with your company check airman? Ask him to write a letter attesting to your flying skills. Baled out the company by working your day off? Ask for a letter. Top performer in your squadron this month? Get a letter!

This approach has many benefits. You'll know what your references have to say about you, because you've got it in writing. By asking at times when you've helped someone out, you're more likely to end up with a bunch of really good letters.

By collecting a variety of reference letters over time, you can pick and choose between them to best support different types of applications. Besides, some folks can't write too well. Now is the time to find that out. No one will ever know whether you used their letters or not. On the other hand, some of your very best references may be impossible to contact on the day a prospective employer is investigating. References written in advance allow you to tap hard-to-reach people.

Before we leave the topic, it's perhaps worth mentioning an unsavory approach to references that for some reason floats around segments of the pilot population. Occasionally when asking for a letter of reference you'll encounter someone who says, "go ahead and write yourself a letter, and then I'll sign it."

Obviously this implies less than sincere motivation by your contact to support your cause. Should you do it? In answer, just imagine the conversation that would result if you wrote the letter yourself and your potential employer phoned the contact (who merely lent you his signature) to follow up. The offer is just as tacky as it sounds, and if anyone suggests it drop the request and look for another reference.

USING REFERENCE LETTERS

Unless specifically directed otherwise by your potential employer, references should send their letters directly to you. That's right . . . the letter should be addressed to your employment contact, but delivered to you. One reason is that most employers prefer to have references arrive along with the application packet. Otherwise someone has to sort the letters into applicant files as they come in.

Another reason is that, by receiving the letters yourself first and then delivering them, you know for sure that they were indeed provided by your references and sent to your prospective employer. Sometimes folks mean well but never actually get around to doing the work.

Finally, when letters pass first through your own hands, you get the chance to see them and decide which to use. Don't get me wrong here. It's not so much a matter of filtering uncomplimentary letters—few people would invest the time to write something negative and then send it to you. More often concerns arise due to poorly written letters, or those that perhaps emphasize the wrong skills or qualities for the position you're seeking.

For the latter, don't hesitate to ring up those well-meaning references and ask them to add a few words here or there that you think will enhance your application. They won't mind; after all they're already fans of yours and want you to succeed. Otherwise they wouldn't have become involved in the first place.

Include copies of appropriate letters of reference with all employment applications, unless specifically instructed not to. (Keep the originals in your own file and bring them with you to the interview.) In many cases, it's worthwhile to submit references even with resumes. After all, good references are for many people among their best professional credentials. Your mission is to get on the short list for an interview. Anything that might set yours apart from the other fifty-five resumes received this week can only help.

Although you'll want a just-in-case letter from each reference addressed "Dear Sir or Madam," or "To Whom it May Concern," those should be used only as a last resort. If there's a job you've really got your heart set on, it's best to have at least some reference letters specifically addressed to that employer. (One major airline actually claims to ignore reference letters not specifically addressed to that company.)

To ease the burden on your references in occasionally providing these personalized letters, ask them as part of your original request to save your reference on their word processors, so that others may be easily addressed and printed out in the future.

Those with appropriate software and know-how can also email their reference letters to you. This should be done in the form of PDF files that can incorporate logos and signatures, and will retain all the original formatting. Printed out from your own computer these letters appear completely original and save your reference the effort of printing and mailing them to you in paper form.

Employment Applications

Pilot employment applications are such a pain in the neck, it's sad that we have to deal with them at all.

Many hours are required to fill out some application forms properly, especially those for the airlines. First you'll have to figure out useful information like what year you graduated from kindergarten. Then comes the stimulating challenge of making all rows and columns of a multi-dimensional flight time matrix add up to match the already messed-up values in your logbook. Those details being worked out, you get to answer global questions like "What is reality?" with the answer to fit neatly into a 1/4-inch by 1/2-inch rectangle provided on the form.

Finally comes the pleasure of neatly typing four to six pages of information, error-free, into tiny boxes and blanks not relating to any Earth-origin typewriter. (Some applications must be filled out by hand in ink. Even the on-line forms aren't much better.)

Joking aside, it's important that while suffering through this painful process you fill out the form as neatly and professionally as possible. If airline applications are still down the line for you, it's helpful to preview some of the forms long before you're ready to apply. That way you can begin right away tracking your flight time in a manner that's easy to break down for the forms, when the time comes to fill them out.

Although it remains desirable to keep a paper logbook, it's probably worth investing in and maintaining a computer logbook program beginning early in your flying career. The good ones allow you to generate reports based on many different criteria. That way when the time comes to fill out airline employment applications, you can easily calculate numbers for the form, like for example, how many hours you've flown night cross-country under actual IFR in each model of aircraft.

FILL OUT APPLICATIONS ONLY IF YOU
HAVE JOB OPPORTUNITIES!

These sad realities of pilot job applications are important for several reasons. First and foremost, learn in advance how applications are handled at companies to which you apply. Don't waste valuable time completing applications for places you'd rather not work, or when it's clear ahead of time that your application will end up in the trash. It takes hours to fill out these forms correctly (days in the case of major airline applications). Spend your time doing something more useful if the outcome of your application is certain to be negative.

APPLY AS EARLY AS POSSIBLE FOR CAREER POSITIONS,
AND KEEP YOUR APPLICATIONS UPDATED

When you can determine that your file *will* be kept alive at companies that interest you, complete and submit your career job applications as early as possible. This gives you time to carefully consider and complete each application, even before you're qualified for a position. More importantly, if pilot hiring at the company suddenly skyrockets, or if experience requirements come down, you're already in the system. Otherwise you may miss surprise opportunities, since it takes so long to learn about openings, fill out the applications, and get them processed.

Also, when your application is on file and current, pilots and other company contacts you meet can update or reenergize your file at any time. Finally, many companies like to see long-term interest on the part of applicants; it shows commitment to the company.

The most specialized pilot applications are for major airline flight positions. As with interviews, airline applications are best completed with some prior knowledge of the employer's objectives. Several pilot career organizations offer detailed information on how best to fill out each section.

In any case, make several copies of any pilot application to practice on before completing the final. Follow all directions precisely and develop each section as you did with your resume; put the key points first and word it to impress the reader. Ask someone sharp to proofread each application carefully for you. (Some pilots hire professional secretaries to type final applications.)

Every application package should be organized, neat, and complete. Include a cover letter, a copy of your latest resume, and copies of any relevant references.

Be sure to make and keep a copy of every application! You may need to refer to your copy in preparing for an interview one day. Also, as your collection of completed applications grows, you'll have ready reference for information needed to fill out others.

Find out what the recommended time interval is for updating applications at each company, mark the dates on your calendar, and keep your file updated like clockwork. Keeping your file active is critically important! Most companies organize applications by social security number, so be sure to include it on all correspondence.

Every time you have significant new information to add to your file, send it in. This keeps your file active (critically important) and demonstrates your continued professional activity and interest in the company. A friend once gave me the following pointer about application files that grow over time with updates. I can't vouch for its accuracy, but it's an interesting concept. She says that thin files are ignored, but that if your folder gets thick enough someone has to hire you—just to get the darn thing out of the drawer!

6

Final Approach: The Interview

Gaining Interview Confidence

Over time your networking efforts should pay off in the form of job opportunities. Sometimes these opportunities come as job offers: "We've got an opening. It's yours if you want it!" More commonly the fruit of your labors will be interviews, especially at higher levels of the industry.

Pilot interview techniques vary tremendously by type of opening and by company. However, the comprehensive interviews found throughout the industry generally consist of some combination of the following standard components.

1. Oral interviews allow company employees to evaluate applicants' knowledge, interpersonal skills, judgment, motivation, and character.
2. Written exams are often used to test practical and instrument knowledge; sometimes the exams include psychological and logic tests.

3. Simulator checkrides serve to test instrument flying skills, procedural knowledge, and situational awareness.
4. Medical exams. Before hiring, many outfits require applicants to pass a company medical examination.

Not every company requires all of these evaluations, and each is looking for different specific skills and characteristics among its new hires. You can see how important it is to gather interview information well beforehand in order to properly prepare.

Thorough preparation always pays off, even if the company to which you're applying has a reputation for easy interviews. For one thing, what's easy for one person is not necessarily easy for the next. Then there's the possibility that your interview will be conducted differently from earlier ones. Finally, a good deal of confidence comes with being prepared. Even in a five-minute interview, it's often clear whether someone is confident or not. Preparation also helps in conveying competence, even if few questions are asked.

Interviews are tough because the skills used for them are largely learned through experience—interviewing! That's why any time you get the opportunity to interview, take it, especially at the early stages of your career. Prepare well and work hard to get the job offer. If you turn it down, the company won't suffer from a lack of other qualified applicants. It's hard to imagine being masochistic enough to interview when you don't need to, but the benefits justify the effort. Each interview is a little less stressful than the last and a bit more predictable. The point is to *discover the pitfalls and get comfortable before qualifying for the interviews that really count.*

Scheduling Your Interview

Worthwhile pilot opportunities arise only so often. And those that do sometimes evaporate within a day. *If you are offered an interview for a good job, accept it immediately and sign up for the earliest possible date.*

Most pilot positions operate on the seniority system; opportunities and advancement are tied exclusively to date of hire. Pilots hired today have preference in choosing their schedules over those hired tomorrow.

Does it matter? You bet! Along with flying better schedules, pilots of higher seniority get first choice of equipment they fly, vacation openings, and domicile (pilot home base). What's more, they upgrade sooner to captain positions. Pilot seniority is almost always established by date of hire, or upon completion of training class. (Within any given hiring class, pilots are often, though not always, ranked in seniority by age.)

Therefore, the earlier you interview and the earlier your hiring class, the better your seniority number. The following story, though extreme, illustrates just how much difference a day or two can make when it comes to interview scheduling.

Several years ago my friend, "Kurt," had the good fortune to be invited for an interview with a major airline. Kurt was offered the choice of interviewing on Tuesday, Wednesday, or Thursday of a specific week. A dilemma arose because of the interview location. The Tuesday interview was being offered at a city several hundred miles from Kurt's home. He'd have to travel there the night before, arrange lodging, and suffer the added discomfort of a strange environment. Wednesday and Thursday interviews, on the other hand, were to be held in his home city. Not only was this more convenient, but rumor held that interviews went a little easier in his home city location.

After careful consideration, Kurt chose the Tuesday interview, even though it was less convenient. Having flown for a seniority-based company in the past, he decided that it was worth the hassle to interview one day earlier. Even one or two seniority numbers might make the difference between domicile assignment in his home city versus some distant location.

To make a long story short, Kurt traveled to the Tuesday interview, things went well, and several weeks later he was offered a position with his favorite major airline. Training class started within a couple weeks and shortly he was on line in his dream job as an airline pilot.

Only later did Kurt learn the full impact of his interview date decision. As it turned out, pilots hired from Tuesday's interviews filled the airline's last class for that calendar year and were issued seniority numbers. Those selected from Wednesday's and Thursday's interviews were put in a hiring pool for the following spring, six months away.

At that point, Kurt had gained six additional months of employment with a major airline, just by interviewing on the earliest possible day.

But that's not the end of the story. During that six-month period after his hiring, Kurt's airline purchased another carrier. All pilots from the acquired carrier were placed at the bottom of his company's seniority list. By interviewing on Tuesday rather than Wednesday, Kurt found himself *several hundred seniority numbers ahead of his friends who interviewed one day later!*

When someone offers you an interview at a company where you'd like to work, accept the opportunity immediately, and interview at the earliest possible date.

Interview Preparation

The role of preparation in acing an interview cannot be overemphasized. Let's say that a company is interviewing ten candidates for four positions. Based upon your own experience, how many of the ten applicants do you think will truly prepare thoroughly for the interview? Three? Five? Certainly not more than seven or eight, at most. If you put your heart and soul into preparation, you're already into some pretty encouraging odds for getting hired.

DO YOUR HOMEWORK FOR THE ORAL AND WRITTEN PORTIONS

To set the stage for your interview, start by asking the folks who offered it to you how to prepare. That's right—call the company! You'll likely be surprised at how much they'll tell you. After all, it's in everyone's best interest for you to come in prepared.

Next, talk with everyone you know who has interviewed with that company in the past, so you'll know what to emphasize in your studies. Keep in mind that one applicant's experience may be very different from that of another, so get the big picture by talking with several people who have been through the process.

Interviewers want to know that you really view their outfit as a career opportunity. This is hard for them to believe if you don't know anything about their history or operations. Therefore, it's important to study the company, its equipment, history, and route and mission structures. Such information is often available on the Internet, and for public companies, through library searches and annual reports. (Annual reports for public companies can be obtained through each company's investor relations department. For smaller companies most of the information will have to come from people you meet who work there.)

When interviewing, it is very important to know the aircraft you *currently* fly inside and out, including emergency procedures. Although interviewers may ask a few general questions about aircraft they fly, the best way to evaluate your professionalism is by quizzing you on planes you already operate. If you can't discuss their operation and systems in detail, it raises questions about your technical knowledge and attention to detail.

If this interview will be your first step into aircraft with which you have no prior experience, such as transitioning from piston airplanes to turboprops or jets, or from bizjets to airline transports, it would also be wise to familiarize yourself with the basics of such equipment, so you can discuss it intelligently during the interview. (One good resource for this purpose is *The Turbine Pilot's Flight Manual,* by Mark Holt and me.)

The next topic of importance is instrument flying knowledge. You've probably invested the past few years of your life collecting multiengine time for your resume. The technical knowledge and skills tested at the interview, however, will largely be on instrument flying. For that, you'll want to be sharp as the proverbial tack! Instrument knowledge and procedures will likely be covered on the oral and written tests, and perhaps in the simulator as well.

Interviews these days are very much leadership- and judgment-oriented. You'll be asked lots of, "What if . . . ?" "What's the worst . . . ?" and, "How would you handle it?" questions. These are surprisingly difficult to answer intelligently if you haven't thought about them ahead of time.

There are some excellent books on interviewing, airline and otherwise. (See Interviews with Major Airlines, later in this chapter.) Reading about such topics well in advance helps you become mentally prepared.

Put together a questions list from all of the above sources, and get together with some friends who you respect. Stand up in front of them and let them grill you with the questions. Videotape the whole thing and work to improve your performance.

Some pilots also prepare brief background packets to hand to their interviewers. Although the better-prepared outfits will already have duplicated your file for interviewers, sometimes that gets neglected, putting you in the uncomfortable position of being interviewed by someone who may know nothing about you. In these cases it can be helpful to provide your interviewers with a resume, a brief paragraph about your qualifications, any awards or outstanding reference letters, and perhaps a picture. Not only does this ensure that interviewers have your credentials during the session, but it gives them material to base their questions on, and leaves them something to remember you by afterwards. Usually the best plan is to make five or six of these packets, and leave them in your briefcase until determining whether your interviewers need them.

PREPARE FOR SIMULATOR CHECKRIDES

Every sane pilot hates being tested on simulators. Partly for that reason, many pilots don't invest the time to prepare well for interview sim rides. This is another area where thorough preparation greatly improves your competitive position.

Obviously it is best to train on a sim like the one you'll be flying at the interview. If that's not possible, use whatever simulator you can get your hands on, but practice flying the *approach speeds used by the aircraft you'll be tested on.* It might be just an AST-300 flight training device with the throttles firewalled, but if you can shoot instrument approaches proficiently at 140 knots, things'll probably go fine on your turboprop interview sim ride. (Remember, some of the other applicants won't have prepared at all.)

If your interview sim ride is to be in a jet simulator, and you have no experience flying jets, you simply *must* do some appropriate training for a good shot at passing. Response to thrust changes in jets is entirely different than power response in prop planes. Without experiencing the difference, you're probably lost.

In any case, line up a good instructor and fly as many simulator practice sessions as you can before your interview. Regular sessions for several weeks in advance will help identify weak areas that need work. Then practice daily for a week before the interview.

Get the interview "sim profiles" if you possibly can, so as to practice in advance the actual interview simulator checkride. These are often available through simulator training outfits and pilot career organizations such as AIR, Inc. It's also extremely valuable to identify the local geographic area of the sim check, and to study the charts for those areas. That way you can familiarize yourself with local airports, navaids, holds, and minimums long before arriving for the checkride. In any case, be sure to know normal and lost-communications IFR procedures cold.

Another useful trick for sim rides regards checklists used by the company where you're applying. Ask a current company pilot for the names of standard in-flight normal checklists, and exactly when each is normally called for. You won't need to know the checklist items themselves, but if

6.1. Sometimes you can earn a few extra points on an interview sim ride by knowing when and how to call for company checklists.

you can call by name for company checklists at the right times during the sim ride, you may earn a few extra points. You'll probably need to learn the names of only three or four checklists for this purpose.

INTERVIEWS WITH MAJOR AIRLINES

When it comes to the major airlines, pilot interviews are highly specialized affairs. It is imperative to prepare very specifically for the interviews of each individual company. Not only do the questions vary by carrier, but so do the personality profiles of the pilots each wants to hire. Access to the latest interview specifics is critical.

Due to the many good sources of guidance available, as well as the need for timely information, this book does not delve deeply into major airline interviews per se. When you get your shot at the big time, buy one of the excellent books available on airline interviews and prepare like your career depends on it! (*Airline Pilot Interviews,* by Irv Jasinski, is an outstanding book on this topic. For excellent oral preparation, answer all the questions in the back, in writing.)

Join a reputable pilot career organization such as AIR, Inc. as your qualifications approach those required for an airline job. (Even at the last moment before an airline interview, the investment is well-justified.) These outfits offer detailed and up-to-date information on interviews, organized by specific airline. For most airlines, members can access everything from sample psychological tests to interview questions and simulator evaluation profiles. Other companies offer interview-specific simulator training.

The best information comes from friends and acquaintances who work for the airline, and from those who have recently interviewed there. Jumpseating with your target company is an outstanding way to gain such insights. Not only can you learn a lot from current company pilots, but it's not uncommon to actually meet pilot interviewers flying the line—interviewers are usually volunteers from the pilot ranks.

Transitioning military fliers should also check within their units for information; in many units, transitioning pilots send back interview information to benefit those who follow.

Internet searches can produce a good deal of company information, plus the magazine, *Aviation Week and Space Technology*, is invaluable when you're interviewing at a major airline or large regional—scan a year's worth of back issues for all the airline news fit to print, including expansion plans, aircraft orders, pilot hiring, and labor issues.

Most people are able to line up only a few major airline interviews during a flying career. You simply cannot afford to underprepare for one of these interviews. *Without specific and detailed preparation for each major airline company's interviews, you almost certainly will not be hired.* That being said, below are some tips applicable to pilot interviews at all levels.

TRAVEL A DAY EARLY

Always travel to out-of-town interviews a full day before your appointment. This will give you time to acclimate to the surroundings. You can get comfortable in your hotel room, get a decent night's sleep, and adjust to any time zone, climatic, or elevation changes. The stress of any travel delays will be minimized and you'll have time to get in your usual daily exercise, reading, or whatever.

The day before the interview, stop by to visit Flight Operations at the company where you hope to work. Introduce yourself as an interviewee and ask for a tour of the facilities. Not only will you learn about the company and its procedures and equipment, but you'll make a few new friends, likely including some upper management. Don't be surprised if some of those people show up among your interviewers tomorrow.

These folks will be impressed that you made the effort to look around; you'll know the latest scuttlebutt for your interview, and you may gain an advocate or two on the hiring committee. You'll also learn enough about the operation that you can speak intelligently at the interview and can ask some smart questions there if the opportunity arises.

DRESSING FOR THE INTERVIEW

Remember that flying is a job of precision. Furthermore, odds are good that at least some of the interviewers will be reserve or ex-military pilots. You must look like the ultimate precision machine! Be sure your shoes are impeccably polished. Buy a new shirt and suit, so creases and fabric will be crisp. Get a haircut two days before the interview. Something precise like a razor cut is best.

The Big Day

When you meet your interviewers, stand and greet them warmly with a look in the eye and a firm handshake. Remain standing until everyone else is seated. When you do sit down, assume a formal posture throughout the interview. Do not lean back or slouch, even if the interviewer does, and avoid crossing your legs. If you're wearing a suit jacket, don't take it off unless the interviewer suggests it. The point is to make a professional impression, even if the interviewer relaxes. After all, you're the one in the hot seat.

ASKING AND ANSWERING QUESTIONS

At formal interviews, the interviewer will immediately take command of the proceedings. Your job is to listen and answer. When the time comes to answer questions, some careful mental preparation is required. Your tactic should be, not to answer any question until you have thought about both the question and the answer. This sounds easy enough but is surprisingly difficult to do. Practice before the interview would be wise.

Take your time before answering each question. Ask for clarification if you don't understand. (Remember that good questions are at least as impressive as good answers.) Formulate each answer before talking. Answer concisely and to the point.

Careful and deliberate answers will help you in several ways. Flying, especially under emergency situations, requires a cool head. It's imperative to come across as a person who thinks first, then acts. Secondly, a wrong or bad answer is virtually impossible to retract; nothing should ever be blurted out without consideration. Finally, there'll be some tough questions. You'll need time to formulate the best answers, and your interviewers will be impressed if you take that time. It's wise to put yourself into an analytical mode for the whole experience.

Safety, of course, must always be your first frame of reference when answering questions. Also consider the comfort and satisfaction of passengers whenever possible in your answers. Those are the folks who make a company successful, and your interviewers want to ensure that you know it.

Think and convey the idea of teamwork in your answers. Pilots with lots of solo flying experience will really have to work at this. If the position you're applying for is part of a multipilot crew, the interviewers will first and foremost be looking for cockpit teamwork. (*Every* outfit is looking for organizational teamwork.) Phrase your answers with "we's," rather than "I's." Always present your contribution as a team action, rather than as a personal action.

If this sounds challenging, consider taking a weekend CRM (Crew Resource Management) workshop before you interview. Not only will it get you into the right mode of thinking for the interview, but it will enhance your resume. "This pilot has been flying as solo PIC but recognizes the importance of crew coordination. He [or she] went to the trouble of taking a course on it, demonstrating a good attitude about learning multipilot operations."

While some pilot interviews are formal and highly structured, many are not. On less-structured interviews, the best course is usually to ask good questions and show that you're an attentive listener. Ask a general question or two about the company, perhaps regarding some recent news that you've read. Continue to follow up with good questions, if appropriate.

"Where is the company headed, and what kinds of people will you need?" "What are your biggest challenges in hiring pilots?" "What kinds of people do you like to hire?" These types of questions are valuable because your interviewers will often tell you up front what they're looking for. When it's your turn to answer questions, you'll be aware of the issues. In rare cases, the interviewer will do lots of talking and ultimately ask you very few questions. That's fine, as long as the interviewer is clearly comfortable with the situation, and you're satisfied that your strengths and qualifications are well understood.

DON'T SHOOT YOURSELF IN THE FOOT

It's amazing how many people shoot themselves down at interviews by saying something inappropriate. Perhaps most surprising is how often candidates don't even recognize what they've said. Many such comments are made not during the formal interview but during the informal periods before and after.

Never let your guard down on interview day! Secretaries hear waiting-room comments and pass them on to interviewers. Sometimes company employees are actually planted among groups of candidates in order to watch how they act informally. Often an interviewer or other company employee is assigned to take you back to your hotel or the airport. That's still part of the interview!

What sorts of comments cause problems? Sexist or racist comments are absolute disqualifiers, whether made in the waiting room or at the interview. Other offending comments are those displaying bad taste. Derogatory comments about military branches other than your own or about other companies might pass as jokes at social gatherings, but at interviews they come across as biases. If your interviewer makes such comments, avoid chiming in. (Some interviewers intentionally make off-color remarks to see how you'll respond.)

Also, avoid making any negative remarks about past employers or about mutual acquaintances, no matter how true they may be. Your objective throughout the interview process should be to project yourself as open-minded, considerate, and totally unbiased. Any deviations from that image could very well cost you the job.

While some of these topics may be rather predictable to rational human beings, others are perhaps less obvious.

Unions and Management. In larger flight operations (especially within scheduled carriers) labor issues such as unions, company management, and their various relationships are highly charged topics. While it's wise to research union-related issues regarding the company beforehand, do not under any circumstances express your opinions on these topics at the interview. If the interviewer raises the issue (which he or she is not supposed to do), simply express your willingness to work within the systems in place at the company to which you are applying. If questioned about labor issues at the company you're leaving, answer only with facts, not opinions. Labor issues, along with religion and politics, evoke emotional and highly personal responses among people. A job interview is not the place to explore them.

Hiring Policies. The last few years have brought many changes to the aviation industry. Among them are changes in hiring policies mandated or encouraged by law, public pressure, and other factors. Anyone in the business will agree that changes in hiring practices have been highly controversial. Since controversy is your enemy at an interview, avoid expressing opinions on industry hiring practices, including affirmative action programs, shifts in hiring based upon age discrimination laws, or the changing mix of military- versus civilian-trained pilots. Even seemingly minor issues, such as the relaxing of uncorrected vision requirements, are best left unaddressed. There's just no way of knowing how the interviewer feels about these topics, even when it comes to company policy. Why chance it?

Personal Opinions. By now you may be asking yourself, "Well, what kinds of opinions *can* I express at the interview?" The answer is none, or as few as possible. The problem with expressing a personal opinion, on any topic, is simple. The company to which you are applying has opinions, expressed in the form of policies. Management has opinions. The union, if relevant, has opinions. Each of the interviewers has personal opinions, as do those on the hiring committee who will later decide your fate. The odds that your opinions will mesh with everybody else's are virtually nil.

When it comes to interviews, the only opinions that count belong to the company and the interviewers. Save your opinions for some other time, like over a beer with friends.

Sensitive Issues.   Some issues that qualify as "sensitive" might surprise you. For example, our business is loaded with enthusiasts who'll do anything to get a job. It's not uncommon to meet pilots willing to work for free for extended periods of time in order to build flight experience. You might think that potential employers would be impressed by pilots who'd make such a sacrifice in order to build time. They're not. Many pilots feel that it's wrong to work for free; they think anyone who can afford to operate an airplane should be able to pay professionals to fill the pilot seats. By filling one of those seats for free, some pilot who needs the income is deprived of a livelihood.

Few will object if you occasionally hitch a ride in an empty seat to gain a little experience. Just don't make a habit of flying for free in a legitimate flight officer position. If you have done this, avoid bringing it up at any interview.

Pilots who have paid for their own on-the-job flight training ("pay-for-training" programs) should also be careful about discussing it, for similar reasons. This is turning out to be another controversial topic in the industry. Some pilots feel that the company should always pay for company-required training, while others think self-paid training is fine. Don't bring it up.

There is a good rule of thumb relative to topics like these, as well as to avoiding opinions as discussed earlier. *Avoid answering unasked questions at an interview!* When you're asked a question, think about it, answer carefully and concisely, then wait for the next question.

AFTER THE INTERVIEW

Send thank-you notes to everyone who met with you at the interview, including the secretary or administrative assistant(s) to whom you reported. This means that, if possible, you should pick up everyone's business cards. At the minimum, note the interviewers' names and contact the secretary afterwards to clarify spellings and titles. If any other parties helped you during the application process, even if they weren't at the interview itself, drop them notes too. These notes don't have to be particularly long or involved and should suit the character of the interview. In any case, it's critically important that the thank-you notes be delivered as soon as humanly possible.

Interviewers often meet with as many as ten candidates in a day. Their memories of individual applicants quickly fade, so note taking, comments, and hiring meetings normally happen immediately. At the very latest, you'll want to write thank-you notes the evening of the interview, so that they're in the first mail pickup the next day.

Better yet, drop off thank-you notes with the front desk receptionist later the day of the interview, or first thing the following morning. Out-of-town interviewees should bring materials with them for this purpose. Even if they do have to be mailed, your notes will reach their destinations much more quickly if you post them locally before heading for home.

Follow Through

NO NEWS

One of your last questions upon departing an interview should be, "When should I expect to hear from you?" (At larger companies you may wish to ask this question of the secretary, rather than the interviewers.) If a week or two passes beyond that date with no news, it's generally appropriate to make one follow-up call.

The chief pilot's assistant, or the personnel assistant who set up your interview, is usually the person to check with. If there's no news, be sure to ask how and when to follow up in the future. Some companies don't want applicants calling to check status, while others encourage it—at reasonable intervals.

In general, large outfits like the major airlines don't want to hear from you often, while small to mid-sized companies are much more receptive to follow-up.

The major reason follow-up is important is that it may keep your candidacy alive. A call ensures that your paperwork hasn't fallen "between the cracks." More importantly, it shows that you're still interested in the position. Sometimes, if the hiring committee is having a tough time making decisions, appropriate follow-up may carry you over into the "hired" pile.

BAD NEWS

If you get a ding letter from one of the majors, there's usually little that can be done. Send an "Of course I'm disappointed, but thanks for the opportunity" letter to the senior interviewers and your personnel contact. It's also worth a call to find out if you should continue to update your file, and if so, how.

It's unlikely that anyone with the airlines will tell you why you didn't make it. More can be done, however, if you're turned down by a small to mid-sized company. If possible, find out why you didn't get the job.

The trick is to ask this question in a positive manner: "Do you have any suggestions as to how I might improve my performance at future interviews?" Even so, it's increasingly rare that anyone will tell you what, if anything, you "did wrong."

Often it is clear, however, whether the negative decision related to your performance or qualifications, or simply boiled down to the number of qualified applicants. An answer like, "We don't release interview information to applicants" is less encouraging than, "You did fine at the interview. We just wished we could hire three or four more of the pilots who came in!"

Either way, you should ask, "Would you like me to keep my file active?" The answer will tell you about future opportunities at the company. It's not uncommon to get turned down once or twice by a given company, only to be hired later . . . if you keep in touch, that is!

One fellow I know called to learn more about why he wasn't hired for an airline job, only to be invited to sit in on the airline's next pilot recurrent training course. Not only did he immediately realize he wasn't rejected for any deep-

and-dark reason, but he gained a leg up on future interviews through the experience.

GOOD NEWS

Hired? You guessed it . . . send everybody a "Gee, thanks, I look forward to working with you" letter. This gets you started on the right foot by affirming the company's wise decision in hiring you, and by fostering a longer-term relationship with the upper-level folks who made the decision. It always pays to have friends in management, no matter how long you've been with the company.

YES, IT'S WORTH THE EFFORT

All of this may sound like a great deal of work. It is! Just keep in mind that you'll probably experience only two or three interviews during your career where you *really must get hired*. That's why the effort is so clearly justified. Thorough preparation puts you into the small category of applicants who really make the effort, greatly improving your odds of success. If you don't get hired you'll be satisfied that you did your best and that next time it'll go even better. But then again, maybe you *will* get hired!

7

Rotate! Getting off the Ground

Advice for Specific Pilot Groups

Until now, the information in this book has been directed to pilots seeking jobs at all levels. This chapter offers some additional suggestions targeting specific pilot groups. Even if you're not in one of the following groups, it is probably worth your time to skim this chapter. The crossover of ideas and examples should reinforce your understanding of the processes presented elsewhere in the book.

Among the groups addressed in this chapter are students still in school and newly minted professional pilots, who are concerned about such topics as how to build multiengine time, how to qualify for entry-level flight instructor jobs, and how to attract flight students.

The special problems of military pilots transitioning to the civilian job market are also addressed in this chapter, as are tips in the use of personal computers for job hunting. If you're one of the rare birds not using computers yet, you should be!

College and Flight School Students

Anyone who's ever been a student knows the pressures of school. Along with homework, tests, and checkrides are family, social, and financial obligations. It's no wonder that many students put off job hunting for as long as possible. That doesn't make job pressures go away, however. "Will there be openings?" "Can I compete and qualify?" "How long will it take me to get a job?" These nagging questions slowly but surely build as each year passes, reaching panic proportions in many students as graduation day approaches.

WHEN TO START THE NETWORKING PROCESS

The truth is that beginning the job search early tremendously reduces the pain of getting your first aviation job. "I graduate in two years. Is that too early to start looking?" Absolutely not. In fact, the earlier students start the process, the better. There are several benefits to getting the search process started early.

First, you can get your job-hunting homework done. Learning the aviation job market and entry-level pilot qualifications takes time, especially since the industry is so cyclical and variable. The longer you follow industry news, the easier it is to predict the best job opportunities and get started pursuing them when the time is right.

Then there's the potential to earn valuable credentials and experience through part-time and summer aviation jobs. These also take connections, planning, and motivation to line up. The effort fits right in with the job search you'll need to do for postgraduation positions. Not only will you make long-term career contacts in the act of looking for part-time positions, but you'll improve your personal communication skills and gain valuable interviewing experience. The people you meet while working such jobs often turn out to be good career contacts themselves.

Though not all your friends will do it, put a resume together and use it for summer job hunting. Not only will the experience be useful, but it's a lot easier to update a resume for use in later job hunting than it is to make one up from scratch.

Finally, those people who succeed in lining up flying positions before graduation reap several benefits. They can concentrate on good school performance prior to graduation, get on with personal plans knowing that a job's lined up, and avoid the tremendous employment competition that occurs every year around peak graduation periods.

BENEFITS OF LOOKING WHILE YOU'RE STILL A STUDENT

Many students think that they can't effectively look for jobs until after graduation. This could hardly be further from the truth. As a student you have the resources of your school behind you. Your teachers and career counselors offer contacts and resources that most students never tap. These include alumni and job listings, access to thousands of dollars worth of industry magazines and employment newsletters, and perhaps most importantly, professional career counseling. Attend whatever seminars you can on the subject and make use of all those resources.

Perhaps the greatest aviation career opportunities can be accessed only through school. Cooperative education programs are absolutely the best way to leapfrog steps on the career ladder. If you are still in school, rush over to your friendly college "co-op" office tomorrow. Do whatever it takes to qualify for the best program available. *When it comes to airline co-op programs, you will never get a better opportunity for a shortcut to a great flying job.*

THE PRIVILEGES OF STUDENT STATUS

Up to now you've probably always thought of your student status as a liability when job hunting. The opposite is true. As a student you have the ability to call people and visit operations that would otherwise not be open to you.

> Hello, my name is Marissa K. Pilot. I'm a student at SCC who will be graduating next year with a major in professional aviation. Would it be possible for me to make an appointment to visit the flight department at Gargantuan Airlines? I'm interested in learning more about careers at the airline, and would also like to speak with someone about what qualifications I'll need in order to work there someday.

Most pilots out in the workforce could never hope to get in for a tour, but as an innocent student—well, you get the drift!

Along similar lines, serving as an officer or industry liaison for a student professional association is a great way to make professional contacts. Volunteer to contact companies for tours and speakers on behalf of your organization. Along with doing your classmates a service, you'll get to know management-level people at the outfits you contact. You're on your way to the big time!

New Professional Pilots: Building Flight Experience

The single greatest challenge faced by new professional pilots is that of building flight experience. While accumulating hours is challenging, some of that problem can be addressed by proper career planning. Be sure that you know and work toward the *specific minimum qualifications* required for your ultimate career job. Otherwise you may lose years on side trips without improving your actual employment qualifications.

For example, newly minted professional pilots often ask, "How many more single-engine hours do I need in order to qualify for my ultimate career job?" The answer, for most aspiring pro pilots, should be "zero." The only reason to build single-engine hours is to work your way into a twin job! Sure, single-engine jobs do serve valuable purposes. The hours count toward ratings, such as the ATP, and Part 135 experience requirements that can help qualify you for a multiengine job. And flying is flying—it's always best to have a pilot job already when looking for another one.

However for most pilot careers, the earlier you can get into twins, the better. When it comes to aspiring airline pilots, hours accumulated in singles rapidly diminish in qualification value, especially beyond 1500 hours. So keep your eyes peeled for multi-flying opportunities! In fact, an overly high percentage of single-engine hours works against applicants for many jobs.

PILOTS-IN-TRAINING

Increasingly pilots are training through ab initio programs at universities and private flight schools, where there is little room for flexibility in planning one's flight training.

However, for those pursuing their training through less-structured programs, here are a few tricks for accelerating your progress. Keep in mind that these are based on regulations and tests at time of this writing, so you'll want to confirm the current situation before proceeding with any of them.

Combine Study for Written Knowledge Tests. Few pilots-in-training are aware of how similar certain FAA written knowledge tests can be. But it turns out that you can save yourself a good deal of effort down the line, by studying for and taking related tests at the same time.

In particular, the Commercial Pilot-Airplane, Flight Instructor-Airplane, and Advanced Ground Instructor Knowledge Tests are so similar that all three may easily be prepared for and completed at the same time. Assuming you are studying for your Commercial pilot certificate and plan to progress through your CFI ratings within the next two years, taking them all at once will save you the effort of restudying the same material down the line. (An additional Fundamentals of Instruction Knowledge Test will also be required to earn the first of your CFI or Ground Instructor Certificates, but that covers different material so there's not necessarily a reason to take it early.)

Similarly, the Instrument Rating-Airplane Knowledge Test is virtually identical to those for the Instrument Flight Instructor and Instrument Ground Instructor ratings. So when taking your Instrument written, why not knock off all three at once, and save yourself headaches down the line. (Again this assumes you'll be pursuing those ratings within the two-year life of your knowledge test results.)

Incidentally, those interested in pursuing Ground Instructor certificates may not be aware that no minimum pilot certificate is required to earn them. Simply complete the appropriate written knowledge tests, including "Fundamentals of Instruction," and report to the local FAA district office to pick up your certificate. So if you do complete the ground instructor writtens ahead of time, consider knocking off that Fundamentals of Instruction Test too, so you can begin earning flying money right away, by teaching ground school.

Accelerate Your Flight Training.   Here are a few tricks to consider for accelerating your flight training, particularly in less structured programs.

The first tip is for those planning to complete both single- and multiengine commercial ratings in short order. Ten hours of complex airplane instruction is currently required of applicants for the Commercial Pilot-Airplane certificate. Traditionally this training has been done in a complex single, in preparation for the single-engine commercial certificate, following which the applicant later goes on to train for the Commercial Pilot-Multiengine rating.

However, in some environments it is possible to use multiengine training to meet the complex airplane requirement. In that case, just add a few hours of additional training in a fixed-gear single, and it's possible to knock off both single- and multiengine commercial pilot checkrides at or near the same time.

Another opportunity exists for those planning to complete single-engine Commercial Pilot-Airplane and initial Flight Instructor-Airplane certificates in short order. Along with knocking off both writtens at the same time (as described earlier), ask your CFI and pilot examiner for permission to take your commercial pilot training and checkride all from the right seat. (Normally, commercial training is done in the left seat.) That way, upon passing your Commercial you're already sharp flying from the right seat, and can immediately begin learning teaching techniques for the Flight Instructor Practical Test. That'll save you five or more hours that other CFI applicants spend relearning all the commercial maneuvers from the right seat.

One last bit of advice concerns training for the ATP (airline transport pilot) certificate. Most pilots build flight experience on their own, and upon reaching the minimum aeronautical experience for the ATP, attend a course to complete it. This is usually done in a piston twin like a Seminole or a Baron. However for some pilots pursuing turbine flying careers, particularly aspiring corporate pilots, there's another option. Consider doing your ATP as part of a CitationJet or other lower-cost jet type rating course. For just a couple of thousand dollars more than doing it in a piston twin, you can earn your ATP with the added bonus of a jet type rating on your certificate. You may or may not use that type rating for future employment, but what a great way it is to learn turbine aircraft systems, and gain a great new pilot credential at the same time.

THE BEST EXPERIENCE FOR YOUR RESUME

The best flight experience for most professional pilot positions is *fixed-wing multiengine turbine PIC*. If this is the only type of flying you ever do, and you have enough hours and the proper ratings, you'll likely qualify for an interview at your dream job.

Unfortunately, most pilots working the civilian route travel a long road in getting that experience, due to the need to step up sequentially through each level of equipment. The desirability of experience, from best to worst, goes something like this:

1. Multiengine turbine PIC
2. Multiengine piston PIC
3. Multiengine turbine SIC
4. Single-engine turbine PIC
5. Single-engine piston PIC

This being said, there are a few other factors that should be considered when choosing between flight positions.

Will the job provide good networking opportunities? Certain single-engine jobs may offer better opportunities to make good industry contacts than some multi positions. For example, it may be wiser to take a single-engine job at an urban FBO where you'll meet lots of potentially valuable contacts, than to take a multi job that flies only 100 or 200 hours per year from a remote location. That brings up another question.

Will there be enough flying time? Consider how long it will take to build experience for the next career step. Many corporate pilots fly only 200 or 300 hours per year. Their commuter counterparts often fly 1000 hours per year. Prefer to work corporate due to better pay and lifestyle? That's great; do it! However, if your objective is to build 2000 hours of turbine time as quickly as possible, consider the trade-off; two years versus six.

Does the job have "step up" potential? Many companies operate a full range of airplanes. Sometimes it's worth starting with a lesser airplane because the employer offers the opportunity to move up over time. Many freight and charter operators, for example, fly everything from high-performance singles to jets. Maybe it's worth a year in a Lance if you can then go directly to a piston twin, and from there to a Hawker jet, all with the same company (see Chapter 4 for alternate routes to the pilot's seat).

Will you be building the aeronautical experience required for future ratings and qualifications? Imagine working for two years as a CFI to earn hours for your ATP, and then finding that you don't meet the cross-country experience required for that certificate. It happens all the time.

What are the pay and flying benefits like? A good income, with discounted aircraft rental rates, may allow you to pick up ratings and flight time that you couldn't otherwise afford.

PRACTICAL EXPERIENCE VERSUS RESUME FLIGHT HOURS

There is often a big difference between hours on resumes and real-world flying experience. To get an interview for most positions, the type of flying you've done really doesn't matter much, as long as your resume hours meet or exceed advertised minimums.

Piston multi time, for example, is worth about the same on your resume whether you've been flying Piper Apaches or Cessna 421s. Turbine time in a Beech 99 counts as much as that in a Cheyenne 400. Types of operations flown don't affect the value of resume flight hours much either. Multi hours flown in a rented twin will qualify you for most positions just as well as those spent flying air taxi.

People tend to focus heavily on building resume qualifications because that is what's required to qualify for the next interview. While qualifying is important, it's also beneficial to build the best experience you can.

Perhaps the best example of this trade-off concerns multiengine versus instrument qualifications. We all know that multiengine hours are the ones that lead most quickly to big-time flying jobs. However, the skills that you'll most need to pass your Gargantuan Airlines interview are in in-

Multiengine job at Company A

Company A will put you straight into a piston twin, but you'll have to look for another job when it's time to move up. Will you fly enough hours? And how tough will it be to move on?

Single-engine job at Company B

Company B will start you in a piston single, but says you'll move into their twins in a year or so, and then on to turboprops after that. There's talk that the company may buy a jet. Will it happen as they say?

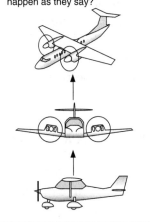

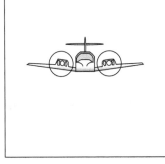

7.1. Choosing between experience-building jobs can be difficult. Usually it's best to take a position flying the most advanced aircraft available. Occasionally, however, it pays to start in a lesser aircraft due to better advancement opportunities within a given company. For tough decisions like these, research the companies thoroughly and call your advisors for guidance.

strument, rather than multiengine flying. As a result, someone who's built 1000 hours of twin-flying in the sunny Southwest may look better on paper, but another pilot, who's flown 500 multi and 500 single in New England weather, may perform better at the interview.

Keep that in mind while building your flight experience. As an instructor, pick up as many IFR students as possible; it'll improve your own instrument skills. Stay sharp and fully IFR current wherever you're flying.

From an experience standpoint, fly the most sophisticated aircraft you can at each stage of your career. You'll learn the most that way, and the distinction may help you one day when you're competing with another equally qualified pilot for a specific position. Most importantly, the additional knowledge will improve your skills. It's easy to forget how important that really is, with all the emphasis on resume numbers.

BUILDING MULTIENGINE EXPERIENCE

As you've probably already discovered, building initial multiengine time to meet hiring minimums is really tough. While there are no surefire methods for accomplishing this, a few pointers may be helpful.

Earn Your CFI-ME Rating. If you're a CFI, invest as soon as possible in a multiengine instructor rating. This is important for several reasons. First of all, additional ratings are almost always worth getting, particularly at the lower career levels. Even for pilots with low total time, numerous ratings reflect additional training and skills. Perhaps most importantly, they show that you're trainable. In some cases ratings will substitute for hours to meet insurance minimums for an employer, letting you squeak into a job you might otherwise not qualify for. This is particularly true of pilots with low multi time. Almost nobody is going to let you fly one of their twins with only 20 hours on your multiengine ticket. The extra 5 to 10 hours accumulated in earning a multiengine flight instructor rating represent a little more experience and a lot more know-how.

Along this line, a few words are in order regarding insurance for multiengine rental. Almost no FBO's insurance policy will allow a pilot with less than 20, 50, or even 100 hours of multiengine time to rent a twin. The one exception normally applies to pilots who earn their multiengine or multi-CFI ratings at that specific FBO. (Otherwise, nobody would ever check out in twins.) Accordingly, you'll want to earn your multi or multi-CFI rating at a place where you plan to fly for a while. Consider saving your multi-CFI rating as a trump card when looking for your first CFI job. "Can you promise me a CFI position if I invest in my multiengine CFI rating here?"

In any case, here are some other benefits of the CFI-ME rating. Surprisingly enough, many CFIs do not pursue their multi instructor ratings for a long time. Accordingly, most FBOs have only a few multi-CFIs to handle their multiengine students. Since the multi-CFIs are usually the most senior instructors, they're the ones who are next to be hired out of the FBO. You want to be waiting in the wings to take over when they leave!

Professionals and business people earning their multiengine ratings are the ones most likely to make business trips out of their lessons and ultimately to buy twins. As an instructor for those students, you'll be first in line to fly for them in their various ventures. (This is how I earned my own first multiengine job—one of my flight students hired me to pick out a twin and fly it for him.)

Other aspiring pro pilots also provide time-building opportunities, when you're a multiengine CFI. Like you, they need to build multi time. When their training budgets permit, you'll be the one riding along for many of their time-building hours. In that sense, a multiengine instructor rating helps solve one of the big problems of multiengine time-building: crew status on more flight legs so you can log more time.

Work Another Job and Buy the Time.   Because it's so hard to find entry-level multiengine jobs, don't rule out the idea of buying multi time. As discussed earlier, it really doesn't matter to most employers exactly how you accumulate the experience, so long as it's logged legitimately. Many flight schools offer package deals for twin rentals, which may be shared by two or more time-building pilots.

If your flying job shows little promise for building twin time, you may want to consider renting as an alternate route. I know several pilots who took on part-time jobs to earn extra money for this purpose. One taught several ground schools a week for two years and put the proceeds into twin rental. Another worked nights waiting tables at a fine restaurant and put the money toward the same purpose. (He also lined up several flight students and some twin time through contacts made at the restaurant.)

This may sound like a hard way to do things, but it's quicker than waiting for a conjunction of the planets. (That's what it sometimes takes for a low-time pilot to get a paying twin job!) Besides, in some cases you can get better experience and have more fun by renting with friends and doing some serious cross-country flying.

Buy Your Own Twin.   Some pilots form partnerships to buy and operate older twin-engine aircraft, then offer instruction and flight time–sharing at a little over cost. While sometimes effective, this arrangement isn't for everyone. Partners must have a good relationship and be able to share equitably in the work, the flying, and the expenses.

Cash flow requirements can be high for operating a twin, and the owners must be able to pay for unexpected repairs when required. Insurance and other fixed costs dictate that such an airplane be flown a lot to be cost-effective. Such arrangements are a little less risky, financially, if at least one partner is an A&P mechanic (AMT). For most people, renting block time in a twin-engine airplane probably makes more sense than buying one.

Be Careful!   Most pilots will do almost anything to build multi time. When you're in this situation, keep a few things in mind. Know the "regs" inside and out as they pertain to logging of flight time. Some pilots spend many hours taking advantage of "free" multi time, only to learn later that it wasn't really loggable under the conditions of flight. For example, some corporations, or their insurance policies, require the presence of two commercially rated pilots when certain executives travel by plane, even though the plane is certified for single-pilot operation. You're offered a hands-off ride in the right seat. Is it loggable? No way!

Be familiar with the aircraft you fly. Don't get into situations where you don't know what's going on. A fairly common scenario arises when airplanes change hands. Let's say that you're instructing at an airport where a twin-engined airplane has just been sold. The buyer, a wealthy private pilot, has a multiengine rating with only a few hours on it, none in this make and model. You've never flown one either, but the new owner is eager to get home and feels that insurance will cover an instructor. Sound dangerous? It is, but few pilots have the willpower to say no when multi time is involved. If an offer like this ever comes your way, ask the pilot to wait while arranging a safer plan. (Perhaps a pilot experienced in that model might be called to join you.) The buyer may be momentarily angry—but offer you a job later!

In airplanes, for some reason, good judgment is often not appreciated until after the fact.

Multiengine instructing can be extremely dangerous, especially when performing or simulating engine-out work near the ground. Be sure to stay sharp on engine-out procedures and to be very conservative in your teaching methods. It's wise to get your CFI-ME training from a highly experienced multiengine instructor. Your students will benefit, along with your own life and career.

For similar reasons, avoid flying for slipshod or marginal operators. Accidents, incidents, or violations will hurt your career seriously; far more than the hours are worth. If you're uncomfortable about where you're flying, get out. You'll get the hours soon enough. Besides, your career will benefit from the reputation of a good employer.

Landing a CFI Job

For many new pro pilots, flight instructing is the first job of an aviation career. Some people do succeed in climbing the civilian aviation career ladder without ever earning a CFI certificate, but they're in the minority. Therefore, this section addresses that vast majority of CFIs looking for their first jobs. (For more detailed information on success as a CFI, consult my book, *The Savvy Flight Instructor.*)

TYPES OF POSITIONS

These days there are several different types of CFI positions out there: airline ab initio programs, university and private flight training schools, and private FBOs. Each has its advantages and disadvantages for instructors.

Many foreign airlines, and several U.S. regional carriers, operate their own ab initio flight training programs. Ab initio refers to programs that students enter with no prior experience. Each student is trained from the first flight lesson through all of the ratings up to entry-level qualifications established by the contracting (or operating) carrier. These programs are sometimes operated by the carrier itself and in other cases under contract by affiliated flight schools. Programs in this country are generally located in the South, Southwest, and California, where weather is favorable for efficient flight training.

Ab initio programs tend to be very regimented, since the object is to move a large number of students through quickly and with good standardization. The result tends to be a rather high-pressure instructional environment. Schedules must be rigidly adhered to, so long work hours are required to keep all of the students on track. Each lesson is highly structured, with a great deal of repetition. Procedures and performance standards are established by the affiliated carrier and are often different from those of the FAA. While this means extra study for instructors, it usually results in more knowledge of multipilot crew coordination than in other instructional settings.

The foreign carrier ab initio programs generally pay very well for CFI positions. One can build flight experience rapidly, and the equipment is generally first class. The opportunity usually exists to move up into multiengine and sometimes turboprop equipment. The downsides are that these outfits generally require lots of flight instruction experience, and new hires are often faced with a year or more of single-engine primary instruction prior to moving into larger equipment. Opportunities for new career contacts in these jobs are usually limited to affiliated airlines. Since most foreign airlines hire only their own nationals, one usually has to network outside the school for truly useful contacts.

University and major name private flight schools also offer top-notch instructing experience where one can build flight experience rapidly. These programs are also quite structured and have scheduling and standardization pressures similar to the airline schools, but with less pay. There's a good deal of prestige associated with these types of programs, however, and graduates provide excellent contacts throughout the country—and often the world.

Hiring at private flight schools and universities often comes from within the ranks of their own graduates. If you're attending such a program, you can advance your options by doing first-class studies and airwork and thus earning an offer to stay on and instruct. Getting in as an outsider is tougher and is normally based on lucky timing combined with knowing somebody.

FBOs offer different types of opportunities. There is generally less flying at FBO flight schools, and often less money than at the big outfits, but in many cases a good employee can look forward to moving up into bigger equipment in the charter department. In addition, FBOs offer prospects of making good career contacts in the course of the job. You may meet someone worthwhile who is passing through in a corporate aircraft. The possibility is also excellent that some of your students for ratings or checkouts will ultimately offer you additional career opportunities.

STRATEGIES FOR GETTING HIRED AS AN INSTRUCTOR

Don't have all of your ratings yet? That's power! One good way to get hired instructing for an FBO is make a deal.

Interview a bunch of FBOs and see if someone will promise you a job in return for getting your CFI or other ratings there. They need the business and generally would rather give the instructing jobs to one of their own, anyway.

Another excellent approach is to bring in your own students. "Hi, my name is Horatio Aviator," you say. "I've got three primary students lined up and am looking for a place to instruct them. Can you help?" Very few flight school managers will refuse this offer. Not only are you bringing in instant business, but a big part of an instructor's job at an FBO is to attract new students. If you can do this, along with a professional job of instructing, you'll be an invaluable asset to the operator, even if your flight experience is limited.

This approach of bringing in your own students is particularly valuable when you're committed to moving to a given community where instructing opportunities are limited. Start lining up some students in that town while your plans are being made, and have them wait in the wings until you're ready to apply.

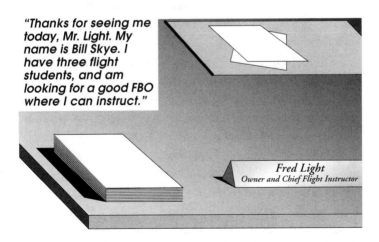

7.2. Perhaps the best way to cinch a flight instructor job is to show up with your own students.

Lining Up Your Own Flight Students

Many aspiring pilots can be found in most communities. These days, most people aspiring to professional pilot careers go directly to major flight schools or universities to begin their education. So your opportunities to attract new students will come largely from aspiring pleasure flyers, from those who want to fly themselves on business trips, those adding ratings, and those who have not yet caught the flying bug but will, if exposed. Your job, then, is to figure out how and where to catch these prospective students at their earliest stages of interest.

VOLUNTEER FOR AVIATION EVENTS

First, you'll want to volunteer for public contact duties at airshows, airport open houses, pancake fly-ins, and other aviation events addressing the general public. You may even wish to rent a booth at one of these events to answer questions about flight instruction. Community and chamber of commerce trade shows are also great places to line up a booth. If necessary, split the cost and manning of the booth with other instructors.

Purchase or print some good introductory materials on flying, apply a rubber stamp with your name and address, and spread the word. Several organizations produce such materials and will sell them to you at cost to promote aviation—try the General Aviation Manufacturers Association (GAMA), the Be a Pilot program, or Aircraft Owners and Pilots Association (AOPA) for starters.

Hand out these flyers at your airshow and trade show booths, when speaking at meetings and before classes, and to people you meet. Don't make the flyers too easy to get. The trick is to offer to send your newfound prospects information on flying. Then you can collect addresses and phone numbers for future follow-up.

TEACH

Next, you must remember that most prospective students are a little apprehensive about flying, no matter how great their interest. People will wait to start lessons until meeting someone they trust. To them, flying is often perceived as difficult and dangerous.

Your objective is to meet students in your role as a professional and an expert. Volunteer to teach private and instrument ground schools whenever possible. You'll find that getting a ground school teaching opportunity is not difficult, since most CFIs don't want to take on non-flying activities. If the FBO figures that attendance may be too low to cover your pay, volunteer to work for a percentage of the course fees.

Do a good job as a teacher, and your ground school students will recognize you as an expert they know personally. They'll beg you to take them on as students! Someone's already teaching the evening ground school? Volunteer to attend as an assistant. Aid the teacher in answering questions and helping students to solve problems.

In many communities introductory ground school courses are offered by junior colleges that don't have flight training courses of their own. Approach these institutions about teaching the courses. If there is no course, offer to set one up. Community college "night classes" are usually approved based simply on having a qualified instructor and some minimum number of students. Volunteer as an unpaid assistant if that is the only option.

If all else fails, sign up for an existing course and attend it. Make clear early in the course (in a diplomatic manner) that you're a CFI and that you're attending the class in order to keep your own knowledge sharp. Ask good questions and make useful comments. Offer your services to the teacher in helping other students with questions. Soon other students will be quizzing you after class about how, when, and where they should start the flight training itself.

Attend FAA Safety Seminars and teach Flight Review refresher classes. Many licensed pilots are prospects for refresher instruction and additional ratings. Instrument students are particularly desirable because they'll keep you sharp for that interview sim ride you'll be taking one of these days!

ADVERTISE

Many CFIs run ads in local newspapers. You may think that advertising is too expensive for your budget, but it's not if you're clever about it. The trick is to go for broad coverage rather than glamour. Repetition is one of the keys—don't let the newspaper advertising department talk you into a fancy display ad that you can only afford to run a few times.

Here we're back to the timing issue again. The odds that a prospective student will see and respond to a one-time ad are slim. Over many insertions, more people will see your ad. Those people who see it regularly will begin to think of you as an established business. Finally, there are those people who always thought about taking lessons and finally get around to it. They'll be looking for "that flight instruction ad I always see in the Sunday paper."

So instead of placing a fancy ad just once, run a carefully written classified indefinitely. Flying is not heavily advertised in most papers. If someone is interested in lessons, you've got a good shot at attracting them under "Aviation," or "Aircraft," in the classifieds. You may be thinking, "Even the classifieds get expensive if you run them every day." This is true, but who's thinking of flying lessons on a Monday morning? Run your ads only on weekends or Sundays. Don't be afraid to ask your employer, if appropriate, to share the cost of the ads with you.

The next trick is to take advantage of your connections. Advertising in organization newsletters is inexpensive or free, plus you have the added advantage of another common interest with the readers. Run ads in your homeowner's association, house of worship, and charity newsletters. Also consider advertising to local executives and professionals whom you know can afford lessons. Examples include newsletters for local chamber of commerce members and those of professional associations.

Finally, don't rule out TV and radio. Advertising on stations in smaller communities and public access channels can be surprising affordable. Sponsorship of a program on your local Public Radio station is a particularly easy and inexpensive way to get your name and a one-line message out to the public.

GO PUBLIC

Another good way to snag students is to go public as a general aviation advocate. Send out news releases to the local paper for any particularly interesting aviation or instructional activities. Ground schools and "Introduction to Flying" classes, for example, can often be listed for free in local newspapers, if you provide them with information well in advance. Invite a prominent newspaper, TV, or radio reporter for an introductory lesson. If a story results, you'll be the subject.

MEET PROSPECTS AT WORK

You may need to work another job while getting your instructing rolling. If so, take a position where you'll meet prospective students. Work as a waiter or a bartender in an upper-end restaurant that is informal enough to allow chatting with the patrons. Work as a caddie at a golf course, or as a clerk in a good sporting goods store.

As we've previously discussed, be sure to wear flying paraphernalia whenever possible so that prospective students and other pilots can spot your background. You may not keep your bartending job for long by showing up for work in a leather flying helmet, but you'll be surprised how many customers will notice something as subtle as an airplane lapel pin or tie tack.

TAKE PROSPECTS FLYING

When you're doing some pleasure flying, or instructing a student in a four-place airplane, invite a prospect (or have your student invite one) to join you. Needless to say, pick a smooth day and a mission that'll be enjoyable. Stalls and steep turns won't attract many new students.

In many cases, it's best to set up a short pleasure trip for qualified prospective students. (Remember that "qualified" means having the money and the desire.) Consider a Saturday morning flight to an interesting place for breakfast. Stick with straight and level flying, and keep each leg to an hour or less. You'll be asked questions throughout the trip, and the opportunity will arise to talk about lessons. Often, if the trip is pleasant your prospect will be ready to schedule the first lesson upon landing.

PICK THE RIGHT STUDENTS AND DO A GREAT JOB FOR THEM

Keep a particular eye out for students who can afford to go the extra mile on training, and who may eventually buy aircraft themselves. Doctors, lawyers, business executives, and other professionals will generally invest the time and money with you to do things "right." They often go on to involve their instructors in flying opportunities well beyond primary instruction.

Finally, as you instruct you'll be faced with constant pressures in many directions. Temptation will often exist to rush students through training in order to get on with something else. Resist the urge! Do a superior job with each of your students. You'll be amazed at how often these folks come back to their instructors, often years later, with great opportunities. *Just because your students start out behind you, doesn't mean they won't pass you on the career ladder!*

THE BUSINESS OF INSTRUCTING

If you plan to solicit students on your own, one of your first acts should be to invest in a meeting with your accountant and perhaps with your attorney. Arrange in advance to buy an hour of your accountant's time. He or she can help you put together a budget for your activities and set your instructional rates. Also investigate which types of promotional and professional expenses are tax deductible, and what records must be kept. If you do any real business, the cost of the meeting will be paid for many times over in enhanced income and saved taxes.

Transitioning Military Aviators

Ex-military flyers are highly regarded by almost all civilian employers. Unfortunately, that alone won't always get you a flying job, or at least, not the high-end job you feel you deserve. Just like everyone else, the trick for lining up the flying position you really want is to have well-developed contacts at the companies where you'd like to work.

One "typical" airman I know of didn't worry about job hunting until the approach of his separation date. An Air Force Academy graduate holding a master's degree in aeronautics from a prestigious university, this pilot was qualified as instructor pilot, large aircraft commander, and test pilot. Not surprisingly, he expected an easy transition to the airlines. As it turned out, this fellow had to work on the ground for over a year before lining up a civilian flying job, and that was still not with the airlines. Like many of his counterparts, he waited too long to start his job search, and failed to develop and exploit his civilian contacts.

START PREPARING EARLY

It is certainly feasible to line up a job soon after your separation, providing you plan ahead. Eighteen months before your separation date is the *latest* you should wait before beginning the job search process. To put this in perspective, one year before release is not too early to start submitting employment applications, particularly to the airlines. You've got a lot to do before then!

Research the Market. Long before you separate from the military, start subscribing to one of the numerous civilian aviation employment newsletters. These will introduce you to the kinds of jobs available, along with the experience requirements. It's also important to grasp trends in the civilian market. Unlike what you may be used to, civilian aviation is in a continual state of flux. By monitoring the action for a year or two before getting out, you'll be better prepared to predict which companies offer the best job prospects, and which will be the best employers over time.

Most pilots transitioning from the military are ultimately seeking airline or corporate flying positions. The best flight experience to qualify for these types of positions is *fixed-wing multiengine turbine PIC.* Many ex-military pilots have had the good fortune of doing all their flying in such vehicles. Others, who've done all their flying in single-engine jets, or in turbine helicopters, will find their experience acceptable toward minimum qualifications by some employers, but not by others. This is something you'll want to research immediately, relative to your desired civilian employers.

Prepare Your Resume and Develop Your Qualifications. Begin work on your resume as early as possible. Most pilots find resume development slow going; seek help from your civilian friends. Military flight time and professional experience, for example, must be tailored for presentation to the civilian market. Be sure that civil equivalents of military aircraft are clearly explained on your resume, particularly where they correlate to civilian models. (C-20 is a Gulfstream G-IV, C-21 is a Learjet, U-21 and C-12 are King Air variants, etc.) Buy and maintain a current civilian logbook; many employers prefer these over standard military flight records.

Without your civilian ratings, you don't meet the minimum qualifications to work anywhere. So determine immediately which civilian ratings you need—then get to work earning them.

Develop References. It's also wise to request letters of recommendation from appropriate officers before you get out. Two or three good reference letters are adequate, but it's not a bad idea to approach five, six, or even more people with your request. Some may not get around to writing your letter, while others may not write sufficiently strong letters for one reason or another. It's nice to have a selection to choose from!

Among your reference letters should be at least one, perhaps from your "Ops" officer or commander, attesting to your flying skills. Most employers like to see letters specifically addressing this topic. Some require it.

Start Making Contacts. Most importantly, immediately start talking with people on the outside. No one stands to benefit more from networking than military aviators transitioning to civilian flying jobs. Even when times are good, personal contacts are still key to getting the best pilot positions. Get in touch with every old friend you can think of who works as a civilian pilot. Check unit records and friends to identify other pilots you can contact at companies where you'd eventually like to work. Of course, you'll want to keep in touch with pilots from your own unit as they switch from military to civilian aviation. All of these folks can provide insider information about companies for whom you'd like to fly. They'll be brimming with useful suggestions. By talking to your civilian contacts early, you'll have time to act on their advice.

STAY CURRENT

Continuing flight currency is critically important. Once released, get into any kind of flight position you can, as soon as possible. Many pilots make the mistake of sitting out of flying for months, even a year or more after separation, while seeking a professional career position. This is unwise for at least two reasons. Most employers are extremely interested in pilot currency. They want to know that you're as sharp as ever on the day you apply, on the day you interview, and on the day you're hired.

Also, most flying jobs provide the opportunity to meet other pilots and scout out better positions. So even if you must go from an F-16 to flight instructing in a piston single, you'll be way ahead if you keep flying.

If you're unable to get into some kind of flying job right away, start accumulating additional civilian ratings. These will reflect on your resume as continuing flight experience, additional qualifications, and commitment to the aviation industry. Retirees should consider using their VA benefits for this purpose.

Pilots who resign their commissions before retirement should consider joining a Guard or Reserve unit in order to maintain active flying status. This may not be easy, but it's worth the trouble. Many Guard and Reserve pilots are current employees of major airlines. Joining a unit is a great way to meet more of these people, remain current, and support yourself while looking for a position.

Finally, if there's been a lull in your flying, get back into it as quickly as possible. If you apply for a flying position while not current, your prospects are bleak. However, getting current again has the effect of reactivating your old experience. Most pilot employment applications ask for your flight experience over the past three months, six months, and one year. It may be necessary to fill all those blanks again, in order to get hired into a true career position.

Personal Computers and Job Hunting

None of the techniques covered in this book require the use of personal computers, per se. However, computers are ideally suited for accomplishing many of the tasks associated with a job search. If you're among the few who still don't have a computer, now is the ideal time to buy one. It's also possible that you have a computer, but are not familiar with all of its software applications for supporting your job search. With that in mind, here are some types and uses of common personal computer software that are relevant to job hunting.

WORD PROCESSING SOFTWARE

Word processing is the most basic tool on personal computers and comes installed on virtually any system you buy. Think of a word processor as a smart, flexible typewriter with lots of memory. All recent versions include "spellcheckers" to do some of your proofreading for you. Some also include grammar checkers, although these are often less effective than their spelling counterparts.

When teamed with any of the new generation inkjet or laser printers, word processors allow you to design and print out super-looking resumes and letters whenever needed, from your own desk. That means no more late nights at the copyshop or printshop trying to get decent looking resumes to send out.

Word processors are also great for job hunting because they allow you easily to modify old written communications for new uses. First type in your resume. Then, each time it needs updating, simply call up the file, make the necessary changes, and print it out. Need a new cover letter? Call up that great one you wrote last time, change a few words, and print it out.

Your word processor will do you the greatest service if you take the time to organize and save each file you create. The objective is to store and standardize your job-hunting communications, including resumes, cover letters, thank-you notes, "nice to meet you" notes, and everything else, so that when needed they are quick and easy to turn out. As a result you'll send more of them when opportunities arise, react more quickly, and improve your performance in getting that perfect position.

DATABASE SOFTWARE

Think of databases as infinitely flexible file cabinets. You can set up each file like a paper form, containing all the information you wish to remember on each contact. The strengths of these programs are in storing and sorting information. Want to call up all of your contacts who fly for Gargantuan Airlines? Push a few keys and you've got them. It is just as easy to print out mailing labels for greeting cards or identify all of your commuter airline contacts.

Database software is included with most new computers, often as a module of integrated software suites like AppleWorks and Microsoft Office. Used properly databases can replace card files and filing cabinets full of paper, all while providing quick access to all the contact information we have discussed.

PERSONAL SCHEDULERS AND CALENDAR PROGRAMS

These programs allow you to organize all of your appointments and follow-up dates. As you enter each appointment, it's automatically sent to its proper calendar location. You can then glance at your complete schedule for any given day, week, month, or longer. Some programs automatically alert you to scheduled events. These programs provide a great method for making sure that you get back to your prospects precisely when they've asked you to.

SPREADSHEET SOFTWARE

Think of spreadsheets as big sheets of electronic graph or ledger paper. The contact tracking sheet shown in Figure 3.2 is well-suited to this type of software, as is anything else that might be organized into rows and columns.

Spreadsheets are extremely easy to use for basic purposes, and in addition to storing information, can perform math operations like totaling columns of figures and recalculating them as changes occur. Accordingly they are useful both for organizing contact information, and for mathematical purposes like completing flight time grids for pilot job applications.

CONTACT MANAGEMENT AND PERSONAL INFORMATION MANAGEMENT (PIM) SOFTWARE

These nifty integrated programs combine many of the functions we've just discussed, and are ideal for tracking your contacts. Most include some combination of scheduling and database functions. Simply set up a file on each new contact you meet, and additional information can be entered each time the two of you communicate. On many contact management programs, you can then enter a date or interval for follow-up on each contact. The computer will alert you when follow-up is due on each of the many leads you're working. Calendars may be printed out, showing all of your scheduled follow-ups, as well as any other personal activities that you wish to add.

Many contact managers even include basic word processing, so that letters and other simple communications may be written and printed. "Mail merge" refers to the capability of software to take your basic letter and print it over and over again, each time automatically substituting a new name and address from your mailing list. Finally, at any time you can print out a telephone list, mailing list, or mailing labels for some or all of your contacts.

Contact management software, along with a word processor and a decent printer, will allow you to do just about everything it takes to manage your career contacts, communications, and applications properly.

PILOT LOGBOOK PROGRAMS

Several companies offer pilot logbook software for computers. These programs work very much like your paper logbook, but provide several useful advantages. First and foremost, logbook programs can sort your flying hours virtually any way you like. This is incredibly useful when filling out those horrific pilot flight time matrices found on airline applications. Sort by whatever parameters you like, print out the results, and amazingly all the numbers add up! Another nice feature is that you can print out neat and impressive flight time reports, which fit in nicely with application and interview packages.

The only nuisance with such programs is that you must enter all of your past flights (or some sort of summary of them) in order to take advantage of the features. Therefore, the sooner you start the process, the better. Features vary among logbook programs, so be sure to check out all of the available software before buying one.

EMAIL AND THE INTERNET

As mentioned throughout this book, email and Internet access have become virtually indispensable in the job hunting process, and for that matter, in modern life in general. Email has become so common that your not having it will actually annoy some people you meet. It's almost like not having a postal address, or a telephone number. Pilot jobs are technology oriented, so avoiding modern electronic communications may actually raise questions about your suitability for some flying jobs, especially considering the pervasiveness of modern computerized cockpits.

What's more, email offers features and capabilities with which you should thoroughly familiarize yourself, including for example, different types of attachments and how to create and process them. Armed with those tools you can more effectively share everything from photos to resumes with your contacts. The bottom line is quicker response to opportunities, and greater professionalism in communicating with your prospects.

As for Internet access, it allows you the luxury of quickly and painlessly accessing information when you need it in a hurry. If a sudden interview comes up tomorrow, you can go on-line tonight and research the company, the aircraft they fly, and even the business performance of that segment of the industry in general. In addition, numerous sites offer ready access to job search information, interviewing tips, and listings of pilot positions themselves.

The bottom line is that, not only must you have email and Internet access, but it's imperative to learn the fine points of using them. In combination they will greatly enhance your job-hunting success.

COMPUTERS AND AIRPLANES

Since you've read this far, you may be interested in a couple of other really important reasons to become proficient with computers.

A wide variety of affordable software is now used daily by professional pilots. As a professional pilot in most positions you'll access weather, do flight and performance planning, and even file flight plans from your desktop or portable computer. Publications such as the AIM (Aeronautical Information Manual) and FARs (federal aviation regulations) are now available for random access on your own computer, as are training materials for the aircraft you fly.

Through the Internet and other information highway providers, you will access many special services targeting our industry. Not only might you find your dream flying job through an electronic bulletin board, but once hired, you'll likely bid on-line each month for your flight schedule.

Of primary importance is to become computer literate one way or another. New aircraft, from turboprops on up, are almost exclusively equipped with computerized instrumentation and flight control systems. These EFIS (Electronic Flight Instrumentation System) and FMS (Flight Management System) installations are challenging to learn, even for those well-versed in computers. Anything you can do to prepare yourself will pay off as you move to more sophisticated aircraft. Mastering your personal computer is a great way to begin the learning process. It's an important investment in your professional future.

Happy Landings!

The Best-Qualified Pilot Always Gets the Job . . . Right?

Right! The best-qualified pilot has the credentials *and the connections* to get the job. As you build career qualifications, keep your eyes and ears open for opportunities and contacts. When you meet someone worthwhile, stay in touch. Do this often enough, and good things will happen to you. This entire book is wrapped around that single message.

You've spent a few dollars and done a lot of reading to pick up that one point. The object was to get you thinking about the value of "knowing someone," and to make sure that you're open to the opportunities that come with meeting people. Even if that's all you got out of this book, your time and money have been well invested.

It's easy to talk about networking and good connections, but talking's not enough. Hopefully, you'll find the tips and processes from this book useful for setting up your own job-hunting system. You won't need to use them all. The intent was to provide a menu which, in any combination, can dramatically increase your likelihood of getting hired. What's best is that this is a system you can control, not a lottery like mass resume mailings.

There are several characteristics you'll need to nurture in yourself if you really want to get the most out of networking: self-discipline; an open mind; and a little blind faith.

DISCIPLINE YOURSELF

No kidding. If you talk to someone special in a terminal somewhere, you've got to get a name and address, and you've got to keep in touch. If you lose touch with your contacts, they can't help you. In that sense, networking is like dieting. It can work wonderfully, but only if you stick with it.

OPEN YOURSELF TO OPPORTUNITIES

"I know someone you should be talking to." This phrase should quicken the heart of every job-hunting pilot. New contacts come through people you already know, and through those you meet. But for it to work, you must take down the number, and make the call. Successful networkers organize their activities so as to meet new people regularly, while at the same time staying in touch with those they already know.

One of the more mysterious aspects of networking is the unpredictability of the results. Rarely do things work out exactly as expected. Therefore, a certain amount of blind faith is required to reap the benefits. "I'm going to make the effort to meet people, open myself to opportunities, and stay in touch with those who can help me. I know that it'll pay off sometime and somehow, though I don't know exactly how."

TAKE COMMAND OF YOUR CAREER

Most pilots would agree that flying is a career second to none. The freedom of flight, the physical and mental agility one develops, and the recognition associated with flying are all wonderfully fulfilling.

The single greatest problem with a pilot career is the emphasis on nonhuman qualifications. Pilots are all too often treated as commodity items. Thousands of pilots meet the resume qualifications for almost any given job. No matter how well you perform as a pilot and as an employee, your best human qualities never seem to compete with resume hours and ratings. Sure, each new rating and hour of flight experience takes you closer to that ultimate career goal. It's just that hours don't represent your true value as a person.

That leads to one of the best things about networking. Having good connections means a whole lot more than just

8.1. Happy landings!

"knowing somebody." If hours on your resume reflect experience, good connections reflect upon you as a human being. Someone out there knows that you're sharp, and is willing to vouch for you.

Take command of your career. Is there a company you'd really like to work for? Go meet the pilots. A friend who admires you? Ask for some help. Meet new people; make new friends. The people you meet offer hope and the opportunity for something terrific to happen when it's least expected.

Make the effort to stay in touch with your friends and supporters, and several times during your career you'll receive a wonderful phone call.

"Hey, guess what—have I got a job lead for you! Just call this number . . ."

The feeling when that happens is as good as making a smooth landing after a perfect ILS.

Good hunting . . . and happy landings!